SPORTS ON THE COUCH

SPORTS ON THE COUCH

Ricardo A. Rubinstein

Routledge
Taylor & Francis Group

LONDON AND NEW YORK

First published 2017 by Karnac Books Ltd.

Published 2018 by Routledge
2 Park Square, Milton Park, Abingdon, Oxon OX14 4RN
711 Third Avenue, New York, NY 10017, USA

Routledge is an imprint of the Taylor & Francis Group, an informa business

British Library Cataloguing in Publication Data

A C.I.P. for this book is available from the British Library

ISBN-13: 9781782204329 (pbk)

Typeset by Medlar Publishing Solutions Pvt Ltd, India

To Aída and Moisés,
who bequeathed their enthusiasm for knowledge

To Angela and Stefi,
who lit up the birth of this book

CONTENTS

ABOUT THE AUTHOR

Ricardo A. Rubinstein is a doctor, psychiatrist, training psychoanalyst of the Argentine Psychoanalytic Association, and full member of the International Psychoanalytical Association. He is also Professor at the Center of Psychoanalytical Teaching, and has published various works presented at Congresses in Argentina and overseas (Brazil, Colombia, USA, Spain, Holland, Italy, and Greece). He is the director of Sportmind, a consulting firm that works with athletes and competition teams, where he also gives courses and seminars about sport topics. He has frequently appeared on radio and television, and written articles for the press, giving his views as a psychoanalyst about topics of general and social interest, but particularly in matters related to sport.

FOREWORD

Football constitutes almost without doubt the greatest social phenomenon in history. The interpretation does not only include the definition of a game with its protagonists and authorities, but also the gigantic apparatus that surrounds it. From the passionate atmosphere of the stands, including at times its irrational violence, it seems to geometrically expand to all areas of society, embracing everything. And in the enthralling intimacy of coaches, players, managers, relatives, announcers, security staff, journalists, public—those who are neutral as well as those who unwaveringly express their support—we can delve into the most diverse aspects of human reactions.

This book by Dr Ricardo Rubinstein does an impeccable and profound tour of all scientific aspects of this phenomenon, taking into account its psychological and emotional implications. Both are capable of manifesting a language, a discourse where unconscious expressions can also be developed or found. And he explains all this in simple and direct language in order to make it accessible to the general public. Ricardo encompasses the football spiral and all its protagonists with awesome detail, backed by his vast experience in the field of psychoanalysis with reference to sport. Moreover, all the topics raised are accompanied with innumerable and relevant examples taken from the sport spectrum.

From the familiar slogan "Mens sana in corpore sano", he presents with great skill the influence that the mind in all its intricate complexity exerts on the physical performance of the players and the repercussions and reactions this has throughout the sport world. For this reason I strongly recommend this work to all those readers interested in this topic that want to delve into the soul of the sport world from an original and thrilling perspective.

Horacio Pagani
Journalist (*Clarin*, *Radio Mitre*, and *T&C Sports*)

PROLOGUE

Being an "athlete" has increasingly become a social imperative in our time. If we pay close attention, body movement, dance and rhythm frequently coexist with sport practices, which take us back to the origin of contemporary sport. This discourse between aesthetic and promoter of healthy spaces cuts across all ages, classes, and social sectors.

In this book, the author shows how the wishes and instinctive needs of not only the individual psyche but of the collective psychology propitiate involvement in sports practices. A psychoanalyst with a rich and broad clinical experience, he focuses his investigation on a topic unexplored up till now. In this sense, this work is truly innovative, presenting the author with a challenge appropriate to his level of ambition.

Addressing sports implies including work on the body and the boundaries of the psyche. Both are capable of manifesting a language, a discourse of disclosure. Ricardo brings together contributions and knowledge from various areas, including news features or popular culture. He makes links from a strictly psychoanalytic conceptual framework, without theoretical forcings and with soundness and clear explanations. He endeavours to achieve an integrative perspective of the biological, cultural and social, but particularly of the psychic and somatic.

For my part, I was encouraged to participate in "sport culture" by my parents in childhood, something that wasn't common for girls at that time. I was able to practise several individual and group sports, both at school and at a club. This allowed me to discover the pleasure of movement as well as a passion for games and sport. I learned to be part of a team, to enjoy victory as well as defeat, and also to deal with frustration and injuries.

The promotion by mass media of physical exercise, as the author points out, has demolished to a great extent the myths and gender restrictions, spreading the aesthetic or the therapeutic and health-care function in opposition to a sedentary lifestyle. In asking questions like "what makes us feel so good when we go for a run or play a game?", the author seeks to explore the interplay between psyche and soma, something which is split during an illness.

We will find in this book universal concerns and particular aspects of professional sport and high competition. The first few topics highlight reflections on movement, competition and also play, which the author says "contributes to insert us in another world, in a transition space where the possibility of self-expression is more allowed, where the adult frees the child within us".

The UNO (United Nations Office) produced a report in 2003 entitled "Sport for Development and Peace" where it proposed to incorporate sport and physical education in the development programmes of all nations, thus giving the necessary importance and publicity to the practise of physical activity, which could be an outlet for the energies and anxieties of youngsters.

Physical activity and sport satisfy in young people their need to grow, their personal advancement, their sense of belonging, love, communication and teamwork, teaching them values such as respect for others and for themselves. Similarly, sport practice leads to the establishment and fulfilment of rules that prevent and offset unhealthy practices, such as the use of drugs. We saw in the film *Invictus* (2009) how politicians for their part have recognised the power of sport, using it as a transforming force in the community.

The analysis of pressures and the various ways they manifest themselves at the mental and physical level during sport are explained with rich and entertaining examples. The over-adaptation to ideals and demands from the immediate environment can have a traumatic effect, damaging both the mind and the body of sports professionals, manifesting itself in the form of injuries as a way of saying "enough". These topics, full of illustrative clinical vignettes, are generously developed in detail.

The author considers it fundamental to make explicit to members of technical staff, family and other participants that the transference phenomenon exists among all players and teams: "… Is there something about the 'oceanic' feeling, the fusion with the multitude that manages to relax many players and teams and make them feel uninhibited, allowing them to reach peaks of performance?". In this way, he explores the intervention of a psychotherapist, differentiating his or her role and including it within a healthcare network that operates by clarifying relationships, elaborating symptoms, resolving transferential trappings, toxic family demands, and unattainable ideals.

The author maintains that "… the emphasis on results, which we observe so much nowadays, measures everything in terms of efficiency, almost as if athletes were machines meant to produce successful results, with those proving the most suitable the ones who manage to dissociate themselves the most, without feeling or thinking too much". I think that we can rightly apply to this book the words of the French educator Pierre de Coubertin (1863–1937), founder of the modern Olympic Games: "The important thing in the Olympic Games is not to win, but to take part; the important thing in life is not triumph, but the struggle; the essential thing is not to have conquered but to have fought well."

Dr Laura Orsi
GP and psychoanalyst

INTRODUCTION

This book is about how to think about and understand sport and what happens with its protagonists from the perspective of a profound psychology like psychoanalysis. As a cultural product, sport constitutes an entertainment, a pastime, a break that acts like a "psychological moratorium". It breaks us away from the miseries of everyday realities and worries, transporting us to another reality—that of the game. Sport represents a transaction by means of which we are allowed to release in a controlled manner the aggression that our culture and environment has restricted from its genesis.

Sport is, above all else, movement. I analyse why physical exercise is considered beneficial and recommended as a health habit; what makes us feel so good when we go for a run or play a game? A great variety of psychological and biological causes (releasing tensions, the pleasure of movement, and the liberation of stimulating substances, such as endorphins) come together to achieve a psychosomatic balance that is both comforting and liberating. The element of play in sport contributes to insert us in another world, in a transition space where the possibility of self-expression is more allowed, where the child within us is freed.

If movement is its essence, competition is the irreplaceable factor in sport. Who is the rival that must be defeated? What does it mean that a football team "has someone as its son"? The representations of the father figure, brother or neighbour will account for the various ways of positioning oneself in front of the opponent, and sometimes foreshadow the result of the contest.

Transference—ways of applying to the present primary relationships—will determine if we feel accepted, protected by the coach, by the supporters, or if, on the contrary, we feel under observation and criticised. Undoubtedly, this will have an impact on the level and quality of the game. Also, the power of suggestion, together with transference, acts upon the mind to mobilise and create heroic atmospheres. What are the secrets of a motivating coach? How does a team prepare or stimulate itself before a grand final?

In this book I ask what it means to cheer and encourage a team; what influence the fans have, and explore how playing in one's local stadium can weigh on the athlete. Is there something about the "oceanic" feeling, the fusion with the multitude that manages to relax many players and teams and make them feel uninhibited, allowing them to reach peaks of performance? (for example, the article in *La Nación* "La ola que salvó a Gaudio" ["The wave that saved Gaudio in Roland Garrós"] (Devries, 2004)). Why did the All Blacks, until 2011, and playing the best rugby in the world, lower their performance when they reached the World Cup finals, preventing them from becoming champions? In the Champions League final against Liverpool in 2005, how could Milan be winning 3-0, later tie and end up losing? Or, how was it possible for the Argentinian Club de Gimnasia y Esgrima La Plata to lose the first of two matches of the 2009 Championships and later, in the second match, turn their performance around against a second division team to avoid relegation?

Is it mere chance or do psychological factors intervene? Pressure is a feeling of being weighed down, like wearing a heavy backpack, or like the sensation of sitting for an exam, which can be expressed at a mental level and also at a physical level. There are internal and external factors that generate it. Nearly always, pressure is manifested during an important competition and has a substantial effect on the level of performance. What occurs most frequently is that the inhibiting factor will operate, reducing the player's potential and generating the feeling of heaviness and the hardening of the legs and hands and a "cold chest"; or it will affect the player by means of indirect manifestations (bad passes, emotional turmoil, aggression, fights, arguments with the referee).

On the other hand, ideals intervene: they guide us, show us the way or, on the contrary, can turn out to be detrimental, either because they are impossible to accomplish or because they are family mandates rather than our own choices. They weigh on our feelings of satisfaction and our sense of self-worth, distancing us from fulfilment.

Finally, talking about injuries allows us to separate physical alterations from their psychological repercussions, which we understand as trauma, and which will be determined by the protagonist's own history, the identification with his/her peers and by the fortitude to assimilate and recover from injuries. This set of factors (not only the magnitude of the injury) will have an impact on recovery and the speed of the player's comeback. Internal conflicts can lead to injuries; many times they are the only way of expressing psychological problems.

Sports and physical exercise, especially since the latter half of the twentieth century, are among the most disseminated of our customs and practices and have become part of our everyday life and culture in a similar way that the internet and the products of the technological revolution have. Doing physical exercise has widely spread as the aesthetic regard of our personal image, as recreation during our free time, and as a therapeutic-preventive measure for health concerns like cardiovascular issues or weight reduction.

The globalisation of sports has allowed the participation of increasingly broader segments of the world's population. This applies not only to participants of sports but also to spectators and the emotions generated in the stadiums or from watching in the comfort of our homes on television screens.

In my case, as a child I took part in sporting events. Taken at first by my parents as part of our weekend recreation or during summer holidays, sports became associated with making friends and the possibility of entertainment; they were activities that complemented intellectual tasks. I learned to play several sports, such as football, tennis, volley, softball, basketball, swimming, skating and chess at the GEBA Club (Gimnasia & Esgrima Buenos Aires), which strongly supported diversity. As the years went by, I selected two of these to focus on (football and tennis), competing at an amateur level.

My vocation, medical at first and then psychoanalytic, meant I was able to successfully blend my clinical work with study and research.

In the midst of this process began my curiosity and research into this field, which brings together mind and body in a singular way; that is, the psychological and the somatic come together but without the rifts that we frequently observe in psychosomatic pathology, the latter also being one of my areas of interest.

Many questions crossed my mind as I undertook my research: what is sport all about? What role does it play in life? What psychological dynamics underlie its practice? As I probed into the literature on these topics, I found the studies limited to the description of phenomena, behaviours and thoughts rated as positive or negative. The psychological functions (perception, attention, concentration, motivation) were carefully registered, measured, and statistically correlated, but I found that the person/athlete was not considered as a whole—as someone whose interior life significantly influenced his or her performance. The interior life was not correlated with his or her family history, the successful and traumatic experiences throughout life, the non-conscious conflicts that could betray or distance a person from his or her objective, etc. I must also point out that if we segment the psychological functions or simplify the intention of certain behaviours, we are unable to integrate the psychological complexity of a subject in a situation of competitive challenge.

Delving, then, into psychoanalytical literature, I observed that this was not a field that had been broadly covered by authors. The scarcity or absence of literature regarding this topic in the psychoanalytical bibliography raised my concern as to the causes for such an exclusion.

In all of Freud's works I was only able to rescue one footnote concerning physical activity, from *Three Essays on the Theory of Sexuality* (Freud, 1905d), perhaps influenced by his disposition as a tireless worker and intellectual whose physical exercise consisted mainly of long walks during his free time, added to the fact that he came from a traditional nineteenth-century Jewish family where the emphasis lay mainly in intellectual pursuits rather than physical development.

We may conjecture the persistence of an identification model that endures to this day among psychoanalysts; the continuity of a dissociation—separating mind and body in academic training and separating the practice of doctors and psychologists.

I also observed Issaharoff's quote that "psychoanalysis has privileged the analysis of meanings over that of action and its structure" (1999, p. 29). In this regard, what has exerted great influence has been "the use of the couch (technique that aims at immobility and distance from action) and emphasis on a return from the external world to the world of fantasy, as a previous step to reflection, putting off action" (Avenburg, 1999, p. 71). The work of psychoanalysis has to do with reflective and introspective processes, which require time. In addition, the exploration of unconscious processes is not a search for a predetermined result. Sport, on the other hand, is connected to action and aims at results. Its timings are brief and pressing.

Finally, we know that many psychoanalytical speculations are carried out through clinical practice and psychopathology and that medical consultations sought by athletes in our sphere have been relatively infrequent until recently. This could be due to the fact that many of them use sport as a way of substituting the mental elaboration in conflictive situations. Nevertheless, from Freud up to now, psychoanalysts have probed into the diverse human productions for scientific, clinical and speculative purposes. We should, therefore, do the same with an activity so profoundly integrated in our society.

And that is how I began my investigation, and the result of those initial reflections and hypotheses, carried out together with Dr Mirta Noemí Cohen, was "The unconscious in sport", a paper presented in congresses related to this field. Even though I had been occasionally attending athletes, from then on I started to help them more frequently. I had the opportunity of integrating myself within youth divisions at the River Plate Athletics Club, Buenos Aires, in 1997, and later participated in the activities of the Tennis School directed by Daniel Palito Fidalgo from 2000 to 2002. There I not only worked with trainee tennis players but also gave talks to parents and provided counselling to the technical staff. Later, I was able to treat professional football players of the River Plate team, and more recently I have worked with San Lorenzo Club, collaborating with Dr Rafael Giulietti and the coach Ramón Angel Díaz, as well as relatives of players, retired athletes, golfers, hockey and volleyball players, among others.

All this fieldwork was expressed in articles that enabled me to teach the course Psychoanalysis and Sports at the Argentine Psychoanalytic Association in 2005. The occasion was very rewarding, complemented by discussion panels. Through these discussions we benefited from the interplay of different perspectives about the realities, experiences and circumstances that surround the microworld of various sports and athletic disciplines. Amongst those present were journalists such as Horacio Pagani, Luis Vinker, Rodolfo Cingolani, Jorge Búsico; and athletes and coaches such as Waldo Kantor, Carlos Getzelevich, Sebastian

Rambert, Diego Veronelli, Nicolas Fernandez Miranda, German Lauro, Osvaldo Suarez, Rodolfo Sacco, Osvaldo Arsenio, and Palito Fidalgo. We also benefited from the input and discussion of colleagues, including Madeleine Baranger, Andres Rascovsky, the joint production with Dr Federico Aberastury, and the studies of the anthropologist Eduardo Archetti. Many of the topics discussed form part of this book (transference, ideals, competition, pressures, and injuries).

My concern has been to express in psychological terms the phenomena observed during sports activities: the way in which mental states impact on the way athletes play and the way they feel about the game as well as the competition. In order to accomplish this, it was necessary to go back and forth between clinical work and theory; a method that I consider essential to validate any hypothesis.

The methodology that we developed over time includes:

- An understanding of what takes place during sports practice and physical exercise, with categories derived from psychoanalysis (acknowledging the unconscious, children's sexuality, defence mechanisms, and the symptoms of various inhibitions and disorders during the game).
- The articulation and assembly of these theoretical contents with the observable data and clinical phenomena in order to create a specific conceptual framework.
- The generation of approach models (treatment) coherent with the proposed framework to address the consultations deriving from those who practise sports.
- Analysis of the characteristics of highly competitive sports as well as the ways of providing psychological treatment to players and teams.
- Description of psychopathology in both amateur and professional sport.
- The extension of these therapeutic models to include working teams (GP, nutritionist, etc.), family and other groups as an integral part of consultation.

Historical overview of sport

A quick glance at the past reveals that in ancient cultures, including among primitive forms of life, there appear traces of sports customs related to the preparation for hunting or warfare, celebrations of war victories, magical and religious rites, or the playful representation of rivalry. From 2000 BC onwards, we can identify the appearance of polo in Persia, bullfighting in India, equestrian competitions in Tibet, Chinese wrestling, Mayan ball games, and sumo wrestling and jiu-jitsu in Japan.

Nevertheless, the concept of sport doesn't really appear until the development of ancient Greek civilisation, which strove to attain the beauty of the body to honour the gods. Their religious ceremonies were closely linked to dance, drama, and music, as well as all types of physical exercise based on one institution: the gymnasium. The cult of the body, which materialised in the gymnasiums, is evident in the origin of the word *gymnós*, which means "naked". In the year 776 BC the Olympic Games were established, celebrated without interruption every four years up to 396 AD. In 1896 they were restored by Baron Pierre de Coubertin, who is responsible for the games as we know them today, involving athletes from all over the world. Rome inherited the love for sports, which eventually degenerated—together with its culture—during the first century, with the excesses of the circus: fights to the death between gladiators, Christians thrown to the lions, and chariot races, also with usually fatal outcomes.

During the Middle Ages the appearance of knights, mounted warriors who were granted an honorary title by their monarch, generated the need for specific training in order to carry out deeds of strength as well as skill; these singular confrontations soon turned into spectacles. The abuses committed during these events eventually led to the establishment of laws and regulations, like the ones that exist today for any kind of game. Fox hunting and fencing also appeared at this time, favourites among monarchs.

The word "sport" comes from the Latin *deportare*, "to move", and from there to "distract or entertain the mind"; it then passed to medieval English—"sport" meaning "activity outdoors", "amusement", "pastime" (not for everyone but rather for those belonging to the nobility). The old saying that "fighting games are a small-town sport" could serve to illustrate that petty scuffles took place in the village, among manual workers.

Physical education resurfaces in a definitive manner after the French Revolution and successfully develops in Germany, Sweden, and the United Kingdom, but it's in the United States where it flourishes, with the advent of athletic clubs and gymnasiums, later spreading all over the world. It was not until the end of the nineteenth century that sport ceased to belong to the privileged classes and became a part of the everyday life of all society. "This phenomenon is no stranger to the process that started with the Industrial Revolution and the competitive ideology characteristic of a capitalist society, which will proceed to stain all sport by highlighting performance as one of its *princeps* values" (Vázquez Montalbán, 1972, prologue p. 3).

CHAPTER ONE

Culture and sport

There is a very direct relationship between culture and sport, since we can fully consider the latter as a cultural product. It essentially constitutes an entertainment, a pastime. Whether we manage to evade ourselves or whether sport functions like a painkiller or substitute of the affronts and hardships of everyday life, it helps us to feel better, even if only momentarily.

Going back to the origin of sport, it is said that "… in remote communities, a relaxed way of breaking away from routine consisted in attending and, on occasion, participating in games and dances. Protagonists and spectators jointly participated in the pleasure and magic of the movements" (Montalbán, 1972, p. 1). This magic has stretched to our times; we plunge for a while into a different world where our attachment to everyday rules is temporarily disrupted by the pleasure/displeasure stemming from the game. Sport thus constitutes a break that provides our psyche with a kind of "moratorium" from the tasks that link it not only to external reality but, to a certain extent, the conflicts of an inner reality.

Sport as entertainment or pastime

Similarly, the function of other spectacles, like cinema, theatre, concerts or musical shows, dances, and other non-sportive games (cards, for example), is to distance us, even if momentarily, from everyday reality. An immersion takes place into another world, another reality, the one proposed by the game, the spectacle, where what predominates is the quest for pleasure. This is also achieved because less energy is put into the repression of impulses that are usually restrained. For the athlete as well as the spectator, it is like an escape valve is opened for the release of instinctive reactions (mainly aggression) that result in a feeling of satisfaction and pleasure. The participant, by identification with the drama or epic that takes place in the game, acquires a more real character, whether due to opposition (rivals of the moment) or camaraderie (own team members).

Those who have been to a stadium or watched a football game in a bar with fans from other teams will have witnessed how atmospheres are gradually built up and that the liberating effect of discharged emotions is produced (in the form of football chants, for example) when goals are scored or a team suffers; when opponents mock each other or insult the referee.

Sport from an evolutionary perspective

Sport derives from activities that in prehistoric times were survival tactics. It is very probable that man started running to avoid being eaten by wild animals; that he learned to throw stones, spears or javelins to hunt and obtain food; to swim when he needed to cross rivers. Whether it was to seek food or to protect oneself from the threats of the environment, it became necessary not only to be able to run, swim and hunt but also to fight, climb and fish. For this reason a period of training must have preceded in order to achieve these goals. The acquisition of such skills benefited a person in the fight for survival and gave them advantages over the less fit. In this context, games would have been associated with competition with other men, and rules would have appeared that were accepted by the group. This constituted a further step in evolution.

We can observe how muscles acquire an erogenous quality in individual development. We define "erogeneity" as the excitability of certain parts of the body, which arouse pleasure when stimulated. Not only the oral, anal and urethro-genital mucosal surfaces are capable of producing pleasure, but the whole body can acquire this quality. Relying on functions like eating food, which serves for self-preservation, the mouth and lips will begin to associate a "plus of pleasure" to the biological satisfaction (Freud, 1905d, p. 182). I believe that something similar occurs with muscular function.

Being able to explore the surrounding environment and gradually appropriate oneself thanks to the exercise of muscular power is a source of pleasure for the body and satisfies one's own ego. Just as it occurs in phylogeny, the abilities and skills achieved by the use of the body and muscles will reinforce, in individual development, the pleasure deriving from that skill. This is more evident in athletes, since it provides them, as well, with a more valued representation of themselves. In this way, muscles provide a source of double pleasure. The subject is captive of the function it exerts over their values and ideals. We can observe, therefore, that in the mind of athletes there exists a double psychological reinforcement for their ego, which we call narcissistic charge: in the first place, the erotisation of the parts of the body involved, and second the charge resulting from other people's regard of them as "other"— gifted with special skills and abilities.

To summarise, sport derives from activities that played a fundamental role in the survival of the species. Abilities and skills were acquired that could give a person advantages over those who were less fit. This condition became inscribed as a peculiar feature and quality within that community, giving it, as a result, a social value as things were done in this unique way.

Particularly during adolescence and early youth, the social value of those who possess physical skill remains in force. Especially in school and university spheres, young people that excel in certain sports are recognised, admired or envied by their peers and can become the object of sexual desire.

Sport as the release of aggression

Culture requires from its genesis tremendous renunciation on the part of human beings. "The free expression of sexual and aggressive desires is restrained to permit coexistence and community life. Nevertheless, this renunciation will have its costs under the guise of a certain amount of 'cultural discontent' always present" (Freud, 1930a). The sexual as well as the aggressive will pulsate and find other socially accepted ways of manifesting. Certain celebrations and orgiastic rituals indulge the erotic, whereas "aggression will be, to a great extent, introjected, internalized and directed against the ego, acting under the form of moral conscience or superego" (ibid., p. 123).

Thus culture interferes as one of the most powerful obstacles to the aggressive tendencies of human beings. A transaction, therefore, is necessary by means of which part of that thwarted aggressiveness can be liberated, in a controlled manner, permitting satisfaction from what is ordinarily prohibited: the desire to kill and destructive motions. This is precisely the role sport plays in our culture. "The pleasure that it gives would be enhanced since it involves one of the *grossest* instinctive satisfactions, those which affect our bodiliness (together with cannibalism and incest)" (Freud, 1927c, pp. 10–11, Freud's emphasis). Sport is an activity with a strong bodily commitment. Muscles can be used as a means of releasing tensions of the psychic apparatus and, jointly, as a means of liberating sadism and destructiveness from the subject.

The majority of actions carried out during sport are part of the most direct or primitive exercise of aggression, including hitting, kicking, and throwing (except in the case of chess, where it's more symbolic). In the same vein, we could conclude that culture resorts to sport to control its warlike tendencies. Journalism frequently makes comparisons between games and battles. The inherent, instinctive sublimation to the game situation is broken to bring forth the direct instinctive discharge, the pitched battle, the war, whether it's between the protagonists or among the spectators (regardless of the emblem, group or country they represent), who identify with the drama that is unfolding.

We participate in these wrangles simply because the prospect of experiencing the joy of success and the euphoria of triumph are within the reach of everyone. We only need to identify with the team and/or individual protagonists in order to join the fray and be part of the celebration (or suffering).

Authoritarian leaders have exploited this, giving strong encouragement to sport in order to unite the masses paradoxically behind ideals that involve military aggression. Mass media can operate in a similar way by distancing critical thinking and reflection, thus dominating and keeping vast sectors of society passive.

Sport as representative of peoples, countries, or regions

There are ways of playing sport that reveal a person's idiosyncrasies; their ways of being and feeling, their tastes, values, ideals, and their particular ways of expressing themselves. Through them feelings of national and social identity are manifested.

Sports can be played according to the characteristic style of each nation or region. And they are learned from childhood, in places like schools, clubs or the neighbourhood where games are shared. An example is the more physical football played by Europeans and the more technical version played by South Americans. Further examples can be noted in the "Spanish fury" associated with bullfighting; the "champagne rugby" characteristic of the French; the haka of New Zealanders; the style of chess played by the Russians; Cuban and American baseball; Kenyan athletics; French and Belgian cycling; and Argentine polo.

The anthropologist Eduardo Archetti further illustrates this phenomenon in his book *Masculinidades, fútbol, tango y polo en la Argentina* (2003). He highlights that "... the more successful players are perceived as models and mirrors of their country; they are representatives, examples of national virtues and qualities. In Argentina, football is taken as a model or mirror of identity. Argentines feel proud because their players perform well and are admired in Europe. I understand this as the eyes of a 'relevant other', which create marks of identification" (p. 103).

The author also presents the gambeta (a kind of dodge manoeuvre in football) as a typical product of the type of football played in the River Plate. This word comes from the literature of the gaucho and describes a way of running that is characteristic of the ostrich. "The gambeta is a product of the local kid, differentiating him from the way the English played, whose style didn't leave room for improvisation, imagination or creativity". In this way, the gambeta became "a product for popular export"; indeed, a product of high quality (ibid, p. 102). This playing style goes hand in hand with freshness and with childhood: "... the authentic Argentine player is the kid, who will never stop being a child; he will be somebody with an exuberant ability, astuteness, creativity, individualism, artistic sensitivity, vulnerability and improvisation. He will also be untidy, his conduct will be chaotic and he will overlook limits" (ibid., pp. 243–252). Thus football allows the adult to continue playing and being a child, Maradona being the prime example. Archetti adds: "Kids played spontaneously in the paddocks, without instructors, as opposed to English schools. In the paddocks, with so many players in such a limited place, the only way of keeping the ball was with the gambeta" (ibid., pp. 243–253). The technical ability and individualism of the Argentine football player stands in contrast to the image of the disciplined British (or European) player more oriented towards the group.

With regards to Brazilian football, it is similar to the physical activities and dances such as the samba or capoeira (a martial art of African origin). This is rooted in the collective imagination and identity of the Brazilian people. This identification establishes important cultural differences with Europeans because, for example, the existence and development of European football styles are not related to either music or dance.

In Cuba, baseball is associated with the musical genre and dance known as the "danzón", an antecedent of salsa. It was conceived in opposition to the bullfighting folklore during the struggle for independence from Spain and is part of the patriotic and anti-Spanish ideology. It was later adopted and adapted by workers and immigrants. From its origins, it was a ritual associated with dance. Each baseball game concluded with a magnificent dinner dance and on these occasions orchestras were hired that played "danzones". Baseball was perceived as a modern and democratic game that enabled young players from modest backgrounds to experience social mobility, as with football in Argentina and Brazil.

Before international matches, the haka is performed by the All Blacks, the national rugby team of New Zealand. It is a Maori tribal dance, which traditionally served as an ancestral war cry, although now it is used on occasions as an expression of hospitality. A performance where hands, feet, legs, body, tongue and eyes all play an important role, the haka is a message from the Maori people's soul. These movements and facial expressions are used to give more strength and energy to the words. Moreover they serve a double purpose: to achieve cohesion among the team members and to scare the opponents.

We see in almost all sports practices body movements, dances, and rhythms, which remind us of the origins of a sport. Vázquez Montalbán mentions that "… according to early anthropological evidence, sport originated in relation to games and dance, although it appears from its beginnings as a substitute for conflict and competition" (1972, pp. 1–2). "Each primitive community linked its dances and games with religious rites, but sporting activities also had a lot to do with the history of spectacle. Attending and participating in games was a relaxing way of breaking away from routine. Moreover, even though dances and games were symbolic expressions personified by the players, participation also included those who attended these events, subjugated, in turn, by the magic of the useless movements" (1972, prologue, p. 1).

Games were from their origins a shared creation; events whose real sense lay in the shared enjoyment of both players and spectators. The theory of value, as always, depended on the uniqueness of the protagonist: the greater the skill, the greater the enchantment on the part of the spectator and more valued the performance. The community, captivated by the magic of well-performed exercises, as well as by the role of medium played by the priest with the divinities, demonstrated by its acceptance and demand of sportive displays that these events served as compensation for their own exclusion. Sporting heroes, therefore, also became mediums, just like the priests, between the community and the quest for triumph and perfection.

It is interesting to bring together these events with the concepts of identification and identity, since they allow us to understand the meaning and effects such events unleash in the participants or spectators, a mixture of sportive combativeness and ritual.

The concept of identification in psychoanalysis refers to a type of bond; it constitutes the most primitive way of relating to someone else. The individual who experiences it isn't really aware of how this occurs, since it's an unconscious process, but it will produce lasting changes in the subject. Thanks to identification we can put ourselves in someone else's place and understand better another person's conduct and way of thinking.

Over the course of his or her evolution, learning, maturity and experiences consolidate the individual. Identifications will produce changes in the person that will make him or her modify behaviour patterns and representations of him- or herself. These identifications will also make the individual merge with or *feel* similar to the representations or internal images of those who gave origin to them, usually the people emotionally significant for the subject.

Throughout their maturity, individuals will experience primary identifications, formative of their psychic organisation (parents, family), and secondary identifications (peer groups, country, ideologies, vocational choices), which will contribute to provide a person with a feeling of self. This feeling, in turn, may change with time, according to the circumstances that the individual goes through (crises, mourning, migrations, etc.).

This feeling of identity (self) will allow the subject to recognise him- or herself and be recognised by others. In other words, this feeling of self is a result of the set of identifications deposited in the ego. And it's not a static phenomenon but something mobile and changing. In this context, the national quality is something that is constructed by a set of habits, ways of being and common language; by sharing experiences and events, by the feeling of an "us".

Styles derive from this; they are a combination of ways of thinking and acting, characteristic of an area, region, nation, or country. Styles begin to gel, so to speak, through historical, social and cultural events that are adopted and eventually become part of the cultural heritage of a nation. All inhabitants feel identified, to a greater or lesser extent, with these common factors, because they represent something about their inner selves. And this is what happens with styles in sports, inasmuch as they appeal to those aspects that become part of a national identity.

We may ask ourselves why national anthems are played at the beginning of sports events and what effect this produces. Evidently, what is sought is to strike an emotional chord, to touch upon a sense of national identity, and thus bring together athletes and spectators. Players unite in an "us" that doesn't accept faltering or betrayal; spectators also feel that part of themselves is at stake and so the crowd gains strength, vibration, and a different intensity.

Dissemination on a broad scale

For the last twenty years we have observed the spread of all kinds of sports activities and events all over the world. The question is why this is so. A great part of the answer is related to sociological factors, but other factors are also believed to have intervened: health education, mass media, the era of "the perfect image" and, finally, politics.

Doctors are important health agents, not only due to their therapeutic role but also for their preventive function as advisers of healthy lifestyles. From the considerations of hygienists regarding healthy lifestyle habits sprang the recommendation of body care and exercise, which in turn has been transferred to different specialists. This information spreads from academia to symposiums, congresses, and papers and studies in specialist magazines.

Doctors, from their places of authority, and in possession of a specialist knowledge, have in our time a significant impact on patients regarding physical activity, whether it's related to losing weight, improving cardiovascular performance, or keeping the body in an aesthetically acceptable form to the patient. The clinical notion of suggesting movement and physical activity as a therapeutic agent is widely consolidated nowadays. From a sociological perspective, one element distinguishes itself with the modern and urban culture of the past thirty years.

> The old habit of resting, getting together and chatting on weekends has radically changed. It's not exactly by resting that people prepare themselves for the coming week. A cocktail of stimulating habits are proposed as slogans and requirements to do at the weekend, incorporated in smaller doses during weekdays: recharge one's batteries, exercise the muscles, take plenty of fresh air, experience life-giving sensations, unwind, are only some of them. At the same time, the availability of activities involving movement has increased, such as sports, dance, competitions, entertainment, as well as outdoor activities like trips, excursions and camping, all possible alternatives to be enjoyed and consumed. Coincidentally, the practice of the cult of the body is resumed, associated to the idea of modernity, whose models and ideals would be related to being young, modern, sportive, dressing well and knowing how to dance the latest rhythms. "Becoming athletic" has increasingly become a contemporary social imperative. And this behavioral tendency is undoubtedly reinforced with the expansion of free time. The incorporation of summer holidays, camping activities, the growing and popular access to beaches are some of the contributing factors that have placed the body in a place of greater prominence. This exposure, in terms of visibility and space within our social life, has made these physical activities a more every-day or regular occurrence. This trend is manifested by the spread of gyms and the use/appropriation of green spaces in urban areas, as places more suitable for all kinds of physical/sportive activity. A further example is the boom of enclosed neighborhoods as spaces especially designed for these ends. (De Castro, 1998)

The era of the image has developed hand in hand with the technological revolution—the advent of computers and the internet, the advertising boom, and the constant exposure to visual stimuli, which has gained special relevance. The maxim "what you are and what you do is not only what's important; what you look like is also relevant" has gained much ground.

Described psychologically, this phenomenon where the visual predominates is characteristic of the functioning of psychic processes where the immediate quest for pleasure predominates; where what's important is instant gratification, quick results, action, and discharge. This is quite different from the psychic functioning involving periods of waiting, reflection, and critical thinking, where immediate gratification is suspended to allow for mental experiences that give rise to various ways of discharging emotions as well as choices in the way we obtain satisfaction.

We also know that "… nowadays styles predominate where not only the visual but all kinds of sensory stimuli (bombardment of information, acoustics) place the psyche in states bordering on the traumatic" (Rubinstein, 1998), since the time required for reception, ordering, processing and the selection of specific actions has been almost obliterated.

The other issue is that the category of citizen has been modified to that of consumer, with the consequent subjective alienation and the states of psychological disorganisation that come with it. But what does all this have to do with sport? Investigating causes of violence in sporting events, particularly in football, M. Halfon (2007) suggests that spectators can be included in the categories of citizen or consumer. The citizen is governed by interests that respect his or her space (intimate, public, and private), with the possibility of displaying individuality and subjectivity, enabling him or her to practise solidarity actions. By contrast, the consumer is governed by market rules, mass media, and the image. Spaces become featureless, leading the individual to states of alienation and anonymity that can be conducive to violence.

We can therefore ask ourselves once again: what drove contemporary societies to intensify their concern for the body, placing it as one of the central issues in people's lives? Various concurrent hypotheses can help us; as I have already suggested, the perception of the body in contemporary society is conditioned and stimulated by the existence of an immense arsenal of visual images. Eager consumers that wish to be modelled on and reflected in them are the necessary complement to broadcast that product. Cinema, television and advertising help to create an ideal physical appearance, showing images of perfect bodies and ways to achieve them (make-up, haircare, techniques to correct imperfections, physical exercise), convincing massive audiences of the importance of being "good-looking".

The mass media has exalted sporting champions, invigorating amateur sports, which in turn has increased the notions of "well-being", "fitness", and new lifestyles. These factors have undoubtedly contributed to an increase in sport and physical activity. Other factors that have contributed to this increase in activity include fashion, which can be understood as the social image of the body (the mirror of a particular age), the so-called "diet industry", and the "Health Generation".

> Understood as cultural consumption, the "body cult" practice places itself today as a general preoccupation that permeates all social sectors, classes and age groups, supported by a discourse that, on the one hand, resorts to aesthetic considerations and on the other shows concern for health issues. The choice of sport, dance, gymnastics and the place where they will be practiced is probably associated to the other spheres of life and the other choices carried out in the goods market. It's true that the social aspects of movement are extremely important: frequenting associations, gyms or clubs means establishing new social relationships, breaking the isolation, daring to confront, compare oneself, compete, join a certain status with fashion and consumption patterns, liberating oneself at the same time from the daily routine. (De Castro, 1998)

Politicians are aware of the power that sport holds. Cuba and China are absolutely clear about the sociopolitical and economic value of sport. I find it very illustrative that in sporting events between countries, the quantity of medals can be seen as a measure of the might of a nation.

> If we categorize it as a cultural phenomenon, sport has evolved, reaching nowadays an enormous economic importance; this is demonstrated in the balance sheets of sporting goods multinationals, in stadiums and gymnasiums, in the advertising costs of sport transmissions, reaching a transcendental political weight. For the officials, it must be evident that sport policy is an unavoidable responsibility of the State, that it will act either by action or omission, but never indifferent to the social, media and economic handling and manipulation that this tool offers them.

The ease which sport has, as a cultural phenomenon, to transcend geographic, language and social borders without difficulty has turned it into a tremendous instrument of cultural interpenetration, as well as being a cohesive community tool thanks to the "identification" phenomenon explained previously.

Considered from the standpoint of social action, for communities with severe economic crises, significant unemployment, poverty and uprooting and its resulting marginalization and social exclusion, integration through sport can provide a framework for spontaneous interaction where personal values may suffer less conditionings than in other activities. Furthermore, the sportive language is direct, simple and almost universal and can be understood by everyone. (Rodríguez, n.d)

CHAPTER TWO

Movement

M ovement is the basic component of physical activity. I will try to set forth different concepts that in my view are part of its architecture and dynamism. On an initial level of analysis, movement implies the body; it includes the use of the motor system, which is related to action. On another level, we observe that it has psychosomatic determinants and psychic aspects, which must be considered.

Human beings have a natural instinct to be active, which is shared with other organisms and which we associate with the preservation of the species. There is psychic scaffolding in place that provokes a constant push towards activity (movement). This peremptoriness is the motor factor; it's the sum of the strength or quantity of work "imposed to the mental by its connection with the somatic" (Freud, 1915c, p. 118). If understood from the perspective of a model of energies or psychic charges, pleasure is produced by the reduction of charges whereas the increase of charges implies tension, discomfort, and the reduction of relief and pleasure. However, we need to generate activity in order to satisfy biological and psychic needs. When we achieve this, satisfaction and pleasure are also our reward, and it's in this way that such an experience will be consistently linked to movement.

Movement (discharge, finality)

That which we call movement could have originated in simple acts of discharge, or in response to a purpose or end (goal). The increase of tension and overload of the psyche tends to generate states of displeasure. The acts of discharge get rid of them. Furthermore, action can be used to abolish states of psychic tension, since the path that leads to an internal alteration is unable to exhaust it per se.

> The affects also derive in acts of discharge. Normally, if an experience is accompanied by a great amount of affect, this affect is either discharged in a variety of conscious reflex acts, or it gradually disappears by association with another conscious psychic material. Let all the series of voluntary and involuntary reflexes that we observe in situations like crying or shame serve as an example.
>
> Very intense affects also require a motor discharge to level the increase of excitation, since the latter hinders the associative processes, the course of the representations and more complex functions.
>
> Screaming and jumping with joy, the heightened muscular tone of rage, etc. cause the excitation to drain in acts of movement ... and sometimes in a substitute motor act of an affect, for example, breaking a vase when one is angry. The excitation is partly consumed and drained by some motor innervation. (Freud, 1895d, p. 213)

Intentionality

When a state of tension exists, provoked by a state of need or desire, this will activate a motor response (movement), which will allow the subject to search for the object that will satisfy him or her in the external world. This is what occurs in normal conditions. All this requires a process that includes memories, functions of organisation, selection and directionality, with attention to the material and external reality, and fundamentally the adaptation of needs and desires to the conditions and possibilities that this external reality demands of the subject. Here, the acts of discharge must be postponed in order to synchronise them with the timing required to reach the objective in the best way possible. The attainment of the desired end will result in a state of relief of the tensions and, additionally, in pleasurable experiences.

Biological effects

The set of actions that we carry out is commanded by the brain. By means of this organ, multiple and different functions take place as part of an integrated process. In its dynamics, the intercellular connections and chemical mediators that intervene in many of its processes are crucial determinants.

> An individual's vital experiences modify and model his brain. Its functioning, therefore, cannot only be determined by the genetic endowment received at birth; the brain, in this sense, is more than a computer, since it assimilates developments. In a state of dynamic interchange with its environment, the Nervous System and the body are rich and complicated systems. They are bi-directionally interlocked one with the other. (Groisman, 2007)

Movement in particular is the final externalisation of a circuit that starts with:

Stimulus
↓
Information (INPUT)
↓
Identification of stimulus
↓
Selection of response
↓
Programming of response
↓
Action (movement) (OUTPUT)

Dopamine is a substance involved in the control and adjustment of movements, in the expression of affective states and feelings of plea-sure. This chemical mediator intervenes throughout the circuit. The brain distinguishes what it gratifies and, in this way, stimulates learning. Concurrently the brain associates learning with the stored memory, exe-cuting action towards the goal. It is said that when an athlete does phys-ical exercise he or she also produces endorphins, chemicals that have a stimulating action and that help to relieve pain and produce a state of pleasure; similar to the sensation produced by morphine. It is believed that endorphins function by displaying dopamine connections.

Recent publications refer to the beneficial effect of movement and its incidence in body systems as well as in diverse psychic functions. Distinguishing the emotional consequences of physical exercise, we observe incidences of feelings of euphoria:

> Some persons affirmed having felt so well when they did physical exercise that it was if they had taken psycho-tropics. But was that sensation real or only an illusion? And even if it was real, what could that sensation have been and what was its cause?
>
> The euphoria hypothesis proposed that there were real bio-chemical effects of physical exercise on the brain. The neurochemicals released were endorphins, the natural opiates of the brain. The activity of running wasn't the only way of feeling like this; this would also occur with the majority of intense or resistance-type exercises. This supports the popular belief that running stimulates an outpouring of endorphins in the brain, which, in turn are associated with changes of mood; the greater the amount of endorphins pumped out by the body of a runner, the greater is the effect.
>
> For athletes, the study offers a kind of vindication, opening a new chapter in sport science. It shows that it's possible to define and measure a runner's euphoria, and that it could be possible to understand what produces it. It further shows that endorphins were produced during the run and that they joined areas of the brain associated with emotions, in particular limbic and pre-frontal areas, the same that intervene in romantic love or when one listens to music that produces euphoria, like the Piano Concert N° 3 by Rachmaninoff. (Boecker, 2008, pp. 2523–2525)

Other investigations assert that exercise influences dopamine, serotonin and noradrenaline systems, at the brain level in the central nervous system, gathering evidence of changes in the synthesis and metabolism of the monoamines (adrenalin, serotonin, noradrenaline) during exercise (Dishman, 2006, p. 347). Other studies have focused on the use of physical exercise as an important part of the treatment of persons with depression, supporting the neurochemical hypotheses previously mentioned.

Corporal effects

The stimulating effect of exercise is also highlighted, contrasting it fundamentally with the effect of a sedentary lifestyle as a depressant and a predisposing factor of multiple noxas and illnesses. Regarding what is directly stimulated, we observe effects especially on the skin, the muscles, and joints. The human body is made to be in motion, and is not meant to be motionless for lengthy periods. Even during sleep it changes position. The body's incessant stretching movements activate the muscles and joints, maintaining the muscular tone.

If we consider the importance of movement, we realise that it functions (a) by maintaining the tone, as previously mentioned, (b) by massaging the organs, (c) as support and (d) as preventive medicine.

Organs like the thorax and abdomen, or the network of arteries, veins and capillaries, need to be pressed, stretched, and moved, otherwise stagnation, immobilisation and ankylosis set in, delaying the blood flow, which will have to be compensated by the heart. Muscle forms the wall of the abdomen, keeping the guts in place; if the abdominal walls loosen or diminish in size, digestive disorders like a fallen stomach, aerophagia or constipation will ensue. Something similar occurs with the spinal cord. Moving also stimulates respiratory and circulatory activity, as well as all the mechanisms of organic purification; the liver in its anti-toxic capacity and the kidneys in their excretory function. In addition, the excretory function of the sweat pores in the skin intensifies, and the lungs with better ventilation intensify the fuelling of oxygen into the alveoli. We also know that muscular tissue absorbs oxygen transported by the blood, which is what burns excess fat.

Many studies indicate that all the factors mentioned above diminish the likelihood of developing health problems, such as high blood pressure, obesity, muscular atrophies, osteoporosis, and depression. "… on the basis of genetic studies … a sedentary lifestyle ages the individual about ten years. Physically active people, on the other hand, look biologically ten years younger than those who never exercise" (JAMA, 2008).

Psychological effects

Babies, from the moment they are born, express different emotions and needs through body movement. Babies use all their senses to discover the world around them, but the development of their motor capacities (crawling, walking) is what permits them to explore and manipulate their environment. At the same time, movement allows them to start comprehending the notions of time and space and the complexities of their psychic stratification. This process occurs simultaneously with the need to separate themselves from the mother (moving away from the primary object), which is a necessary activity for psychological development. This psychic commotion will be an intense source of pleasure (and at the same time of pain), which will allow the infant to affirm himself, gradually developing independence and autonomy as well as self-esteem, a result of the achievements and accomplishments obtained.

In adult life, movement is used, as mentioned, to obtain that which we desire, struggling until it is obtained. But it's also frequently used in unpleasant or dangerous situations to distance oneself from peril. The saying "he who fights and runs away will live to fight another day" is very true. Taking psychological distance from experiences of a toxic or absorbing nature is not as easily accomplished as the motor reflex of getting away. For old people and those in a depressive state, moving serves to avoid experiences of stasis and death (physical and psychological). In both cases, a feeling of power and control is enjoyed. "The latter helps to diminish the sensation of helplessness, without nullifying it, and counteracts lack of psychic control" (Alizade, 1996, pp. 9–16).

In the Freudian sense sport is used as a way of distancing the young from sexual activity, substituting it for the pleasure of movement. Movement, in fact, takes us back to a kind of satisfaction that we categorise as self-erotic; that is, a way of obtaining pleasure alone through the stimulation of sensations or parts of the body.

Passive pleasure

Passive pleasure is linked to auto-eroticism. The idea of a total object as a source of pleasure doesn't exist in this case. We can find this form of pleasure in the repetition of mechanical movements (for example, in being rocked to sleep travelling by car or train). Likewise, many adults and children find the movement of rides (such as roller coasters) conducive to pleasure. The feeling of falling and weightlessness produced by parachuting and hang-gliding can be another source of passive pleasure, as is letting ourselves be carried along by the current when in water, or experiencing the motion of playground swings and slides.

The therapeutic effect that repetitive movement can have is significant for persons with physical disabilities, the elderly, or persons with severe disturbances in their body schema. I'll take the example of Florence, a thirty-year-old overweight woman who had so much anger and rejection aimed towards her own body that she found it impossible to perceive it as a source of pleasure. This led to a serious withdrawal from her social environment and affected her love life. Florence told me during her therapy sessions that she felt her body was only capable of causing her worries, serving as an object of medical measurements and investigations, which annoyed her.

During the course of the analytical process and remembering situations from her past, we found that during her childhood she had enjoyed playing on the swings. Working with this pleasant memory, I suggested that she make a swing that could hold and contain her in order to reproduce once again those pleasurable sensations. It was not an easy task to move forward with, since she built a series of defences and rationalisations that prevented her from connecting herself to her desires and passive pleasure. After a few months, she complied to building her swing and, despite the fear of ridicule and the shame produced by being observed by her neighbours, she was slowly able to start enjoying this source of pleasure, derived from her body and its sensitivity. This enabled her to confront the voracity of her negative inner monologue that perpetuated her symptoms. In addition, alternative ways of relating to her family members also developed, since she was able to treat the source of her illness and upset and was subsequently able to play and laugh as she hadn't done in a long time.

Active pleasure

Active pleasure is related to the experiences that provide for the control and management of one's own body. In this regard, the auto-perception of the body, as the factor relating a person to his environment, forms a person's idea of himself, separating him from the initial symbiosis with the mother. This transition from dependency to autonomy, from passivity to activity, from auto-erotic pleasure to narcissism, is found and rediscovered each time we voluntarily use the body and muscles to attain an end or goal. Being able to exercise gives us a sense of power and sufficiency, which is very pleasant and comforting. It influences the idea we have of ourselves as capable of achieving goals, which generates an experience of self-esteem, concurrent with a powerful and positive sense of self-worth. This mechanism of auto-observation and evaluation is what will promote what we call self-esteem. And this is what will increase with the proof of sufficiency.

As the child proceeds to affirm himself via the conquest of persons and objects that surround him, "the child mentally allows his illusion of unlimited power to grow (child omnipotence); this illusion begins to establish itself, not as it tries to fusion with those persons and objects but when it manages to eliminate their resistance to its attacks" (Del Valle Echegaray & Moise de Borgnia, 1996). In being self-assertive "there is an aspiration *to expand at the expense of others*. But this doesn't occur just to subject them in order to satisfy a need or desire, but also to be recognized" (Green, 1986, p. 67).

At present we can observe that in many athletic disciplines the emphasis is placed on participation and achieving goals. Kathy, Mary, and Sylvia, runners of a city marathon on Women's Day, expressed themselves thus when asked why they had participated: "it's a challenge, and we proved to ourselves that we can do it, we aren't so concerned about arriving, being first or running many kilometres but about being able to participate and enjoy this event".

Pacher (28), a lifeguard, pointed out:

> ... I run, but not because I necessarily like it. I do it because it's an aerobic workout, and if I can keep a certain rhythm for a long time I can perform better when I swim. It gives me greater strength in the legs and more oxygen. I walk and I jog because it's good for the circulation. Trainers say it and it's also recommended for the elderly, those who have varicose veins, and people who are overweight. I know that if they do it for more than half an hour, they burn fat and the body's weight doesn't have such an impact on the knees. I move because it gives me pleasure. Swimming, for example, gives me great satisfaction. I do an exercise, perform it well and it's good for my body. I feel proud, happy of having been able to do it. To achieve it is to fulfil a goal. I also swim to keep fit. It gives me pleasure, it relaxes me; my thoughts are directed towards pleasant places, like what I'm going to wear in the evening or something tasty that I'll cook later. Some people do exercise or swim because they are angry. When they swim, they kill the ogre. I went for a swim after a fight; I killed the water and got rid of my anger.

The body is left relaxed, and so is the head ... but this is not a therapy. At other times it's useful to make new and different thought connections. It's fun ...

A growing number of people get together to do aerobic activity. Even if some people do it on their own, group activity adds to the possibility of developing emotional ties with others and a sense of belonging. Perhaps this is one of the reasons that explains the boom in physical activity. This phenomenon has been growing simultaneously with the recommendations by doctors and nutritionists as well as the companies advertising and promoting sportswear, who see an attractive market in the expansion of these practices.

There are other activities and sports involving the management and control of a machine, instrument, or animal. In these cases, the pleasure stems from the skill in carrying out the activity (we can see this in motor racing, canoeing, rafting, cycling, horse riding, and polo). The knowledge of one's own skill and the power to carry it out go hand in hand to increase self-esteem and a sense of autonomy.

Competition, first and foremost, is with oneself, with the challenge of proving and demonstrating that one is competent and capable; winning against an opponent is a plus. For these reasons, it's commonly affirmed that physical exercise has a strong anti-depressive effect (if met successfully) and is a beneficial stimulus for a person's self-esteem (as has already been shown).

In the light of these concepts I must point out that in recommending exercise to a patient or athlete, options must be explored and regulated, particularly in those persons whose self-esteem and psychological resources are very weak, and who are searching to recompose and heal psychological wounds. It is no minor point to reaffirm that the experience of self-mastery diminishes the sensation of helplessness, lowers anguish, relieves any internal conflicts, and diverts attention from psychic pain, but in no way annuls or makes it disappear. Another element that we must pay attention to is the motor system. Muscles are not only used for movement but also for energy discharge and are a source of eroticism and a form of language and expression. They take the place of an efferent channel that releases products of the internal world. Even if the movement of muscles is the final channel of the process, it follows on from psychological complexity and stratification as well as mental development and maturity.

At a level of rudimentary psychic constitution, muscles are used only for the purpose of discharge, almost like in the model of the reflex act. This implies the evacuation of the energy contributed to the psychic apparatus by excitations. Another internal channel of derivation is the innervations that manifest as mimicry or expression of affect. In all cases, discharge is the result of the inability to tolerate the growth of tension that can turn into anguish or somatic symptoms.

A level of greater development will occur between the stimulus and the reaction thanks to the acquisition of a tolerance capacity of the tension. This capacity is sought by thought, which on the one hand suspends the motor discharge and on the other hand requires the transport of freely moveable energy to linked energy. The attachment implies that a determined psychic energy is "tied" to a single representation, a group of representations, a part of the body, or an object. This substitutes the simple discharge reactions for more complex acts. As we begin to advance, the capacity to observe, select and organise stimuli and impulses increases. This occurs by representing, thinking and later judging, with the intervention of the principle of reality.

The case of Anthony

Let's explore what happened with Anthony, a forty-two-year-old patient. Anthony is referred to therapy by his general practitioner because he experiences very intense muscular spasms, diagnosed as a tetany crisis. An ex-player of first division volleyball, he practises during weekends at a club, combining it with some golf. Anthony is initially unwilling to admit that what is happening to him has anything to do with his psyche. Nevertheless, during the course of the sessions he says that he finds himself in a state of unbearable tension, the result of his work and family situation: he's debt ridden, and feels hostility, resentment and impotence, not only because he must admit to an abrupt reduction of his standard of living (lower salary) but because he feels diminished before colleagues and friends (managers of firms). The muscular discharges, somatic derivations of affects and representations that he cannot process lead him to have to deal with his crisis.

Anthony is a man of few words. He's used to pragmatic and motor action where business and sport are his favourite channels. We know that an important step in psychological evolution is the possibility of thought linked to words, and its anticipatory capacity. Thinking is hard for Anthony. This difficulty with verbal expression is common in many athletes, in contrast to the possibility of expressing themselves through the language of action, using the motor apparatus.

During the therapy sessions, Anthony's discourse is cathartic. His account reproduces sensory impressions and emotional experiences that haven't been transformed—psychically worked out—and therefore he is not ready to think or dream about them or analyse them. These elements are lived as "things in themselves" and generally are unrecognised by the subject as coming from himself; they are identified in others rather than in himself. In one of the sessions, the following dialogue takes place:

Anthony: What I really wish is not to have muscular crises anymore, but I'd rather talk about business or holes under par.

Analyst: And not have to feel anything?

Anthony: What for? So that it will hurt, so that my brain will explode?

Analyst: Precisely, because being able to talk about your pain means we can contain it and it doesn't explode.

Putting a name and words to affects, establishing connections with relevant ideas and, in the here and now of the transference, getting Anthony to recognise and connect with what emerges from his inner self is a very slow task. He wants others to take care of that which he cannot manage, including the payment of his therapy, which he attends on a daily basis: "I pass on the invoice to the company as occupational illness; they were the cause of it". For this reason, it's a significant milestone in the therapy process when he begins to pay the treatment fees. Fears of becoming addicted to therapy arise later on; it is a dependency that he experiences as subjection.

Slowly Anthony begins to realise that his muscles have functioned as a shield, a "shell" as he puts it, in which he has been sustaining, through action and athletic success (winning against other men), the need for assertion of his manliness. These ideals (success and action) are promoted by the very culture of our time.

Psychosomatic aspects

In cases like that of Anthony's, there is opposition between processes that search to unify affects, representations, fantasies and generate thought, and those that seek relief, evacuation and discharge through the muscles.

There's a common saying that opposes muscles in favour of brains. We ask ourselves, therefore, if only the muscular discharge operates in those who practise sport. And the brain? If we observe this closely, we can see that to perform well in a game involves a complex mechanism of psycho-motor synchronisation—tactics and strategies that denote certain types of thought for which a charge and ideo-affective ties are required. And this would appear to oppose what has been previously affirmed.

The Psychosomatic School of Paris described a way of thinking characterised by investiture processes of an archaic level precariously connected with words: operational thinking (Marty, 1963, pp. 449–459). If this model is taken into consideration we could overcome the apparent contradiction. But even if thought during athletic activity is oriented towards external (rather than internal) sensitive reality and is rich in automatic behaviours, it presents some differences.

It can be said that during athletic activity thought adopts an operational quality, since: (a) it has a low level of charge or investiture; (b) it's oriented towards the exterior; and (c) therefore orientation towards the sense organs predominates over the interoceptive. Nevertheless, and in contrast with the latter point, thoughts during sport activity contain a greater network of fantasies linked to them as well as possibilities of instinctive satisfaction during the game.

With professional athletes we observe more operability in high competition, where the acquisition of automatisms is manifested with greater clarity. For many athletes, the connection with their emotional states is an undesirable interference, since it disconnects them from the development of the game. Another factor that would be altered here is the pre-eminence of the pleasure principle (playing for enjoyment) over the reality principle (playing to win). What's more, they transform themselves into hyperrealists.

The demands of the competitive situation and the pressure to obtain a successful result, which bring as a corollary important gratifications for the ego as well as material benefits, lead many athletes to a situation of over-adaptation. Injuries and in some cases addictions would signal protest against these demands. Here we would find ourselves in a situation diametrically opposed to sport as a game. On the other hand, many persons practise sport in search of relief from the states of tension they suffer. In contrast to other athletes, their greater disconnection with the corporal and interoceptive can lead them to serious accidents, either sportive or somatic (sudden death). The game, for them, becomes a new task that they are forced to fulfil. Lastly, at the psychological level, the idea of action is frequently associated with discharge, which in turn has been linked to incapacity or psychic immaturity.

Appealing to a model where body, mind and the exterior world interact as spaces of expression, we can observe that when the processing of experiences and affects in the mental field is surpassed, the subject channels expression through his or her body (including in some cases, bodily illness) or through certain behaviours or forms of conduct.

In contrast with the approaches centred in pathology, some authors raise the idea of psychosomatic integration as a developmental achievement ("healthy development") and the pleasure of psychosomatic unity in experience (Winnicott, 1969, pp. 205–216). During movement, a particular interplay of psyche-soma takes place, as opposed to a division of the two, which occurs during illness. Even though in both cases that which is mental remains separate (there is a kind of suspension of the processes of reflection, fantasy, and daydream), we see a deeper split between the two mechanisms in those who suffer some pathology. If we interpret the process of becoming ill as a rupture in the "psychosomatic equilibrium", the process generated by movement would have a homeostatic function—that is, of regulation and harmony in support of the above-mentioned equilibrium. For others, "certain body experiences, for example, an evening headache after an intense day's work, would be the corporal expression of a momentary disorganization due to failures in the psychic system to process traumatic situations" (D'Alvia, 1995, p. 126). Lastly, there are those who maintain that "the body would act as a buffer, a kind of protector of the mental level when a certain threshold of tolerance of the psyche is exceeded" (Bleger, 1978, p. 24).

Unlike these three approaches, I would suggest that more than a passage *to* the body, this would involve a passage *through* the body. Perhaps the usual recommendation of "doing exercise because it's healthy" implies the idea of protection, a defence against disorganised mental processes that will involve the somatic. In this regard, movement would act as an intermediary defence against psychosomatic illness.

The appropriation of motor discharge would be a similar act of defence, but the autonomous nervous system (sympathetic and parasympathetic system) and the internal body organs would mainly intervene, producing somatic illness. In "normal" movement, the whole body may participate, especially the musculoskeletal system, and the discharge is led towards the exterior. We can say that doing exercise, moving, "re-charges the batteries" or that "walking helps to clear one's head". How can we understand this within this scheme?

If we understood movement as a discharge phenomenon liberating the mental (ideas, affects), particularly those with negative or destructive contents, and thus having a liberating, revitalising and clarifying effect, we would be thinking in a similar way to that of our primitive ancestors (magic, omnipotence of ideas), who believed that when we move, when we discharge the muscles, we expel outwards everything that is toxic and harmful to our mind. "This phenomenon isn't only energetic discharge but also includes a way of channelling and manifesting contents of the internal world, as well as symbolically acting out the fantasies" (Baranger & Baranger, 1993, p. 72). Simultaneously, at the ideational level, the stimulating and pleasurable effect that comes from movement provides a kind of energetic recharge that will expand from the corporal base to include the whole subject.

Summary

In the following figures we sum up the concepts expressed in this chapter.

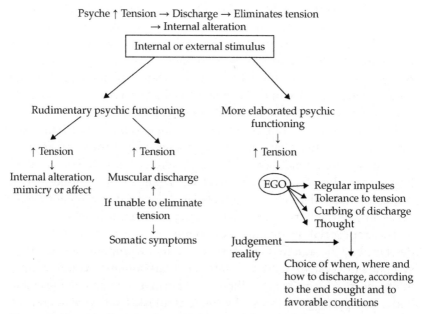

Figure 1. Psychic functioning, tension, and forms of discharge.

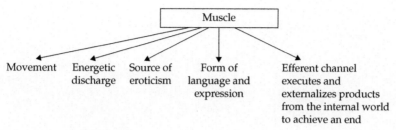

Figure 2. Muscle functions.

Instinct to be active (biological) → Preservation of life (life instincts)
Eros → Drive → Push (constant, peremptory) → Movement (demand of psychic work)

We find a multi-causality in obtaining pleasure through movement

A) Movement   →   Discharge of tensions → Relief → Pleasure
                           Satisfaction of need → Relief → Pleasure
B) Biological effects   →   Liberation of stimulating substances
                           (dopamine, endorphins)
C) Bodily effects   →   Keeps muscular tone
                           Support
                           Organic massage
                           Preventive (of sedentary lifestyle and its effects, muscular
                           atrophy, blood stasis, ankylosis, aging)
D) Psychic effects
       1) General
       2) Developmentally (in the child → separating from the mother → growing,
           maturing)
       3) Adult → To get away from toxic situations both physical and psycholaogical
       4) By the type of pleasure
               a) Passive is more auto-erotic → Rocking, letting oneself fall (swing, slide,
                                       hang-glide, parachute, raft, canoe)
               b) Active   → Experiences of management and control in
                                       relation to the environment and others
               c) Mixed
E) Psychosomatic aspects
       1) Effect of rebalancing   →   Discharge of the mental (toxic)
                                               ↓
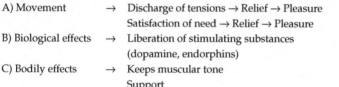
                           Recharge from body source (energetic)
                           Revitalising and clarifying effect
       2) Protects psychosomatic equilibrium   →   Acts as an intermediary
                                                       defence before illness

Figure 3. Movement effects.

CHAPTER THREE

Play

In order to understand the ludic elements of sport, and play itself, we have an extensive bibliography at our disposal, which, although mainly refers to the understanding of play in children, provides us with observations that can also be applied to adults. An initial definition asserts that "Play is not just a mental activity but also involves the body's participation. It takes place at an external time and space. In play, both the external and the internal coexist" (Winnicott, 1972, pp. 38–52).

Amongst young animals and children, play occupies an important learning and exploration function not only of their own capacities and abilities but also in relation to the environment. In fact, play seems to be fundamentally at the service of the struggle for survival. It's a way of "starting to train". Play is also a way of expressing fantasies and processing traumatic situations, transforming what is experienced passively into something active. Play occurs "in health", since, to a certain extent, it implies getting away from self-absorption and connecting with others. As the following example illustrates: "… schizophrenic children are not able to play in the true sense of the word. They can only perform certain monotonous actions. On the other hand, neurotic children play at giving life or imagining characters that are a projection of their internal world. These mechanisms provoke relief from inner anguish, since through personification they are placed 'outside' (they project themselves) and can be treated, in part, as a non-ego, some aspects of themselves as if they were other people's" (Klein, 1929, pp. 193–204). In this way, the liberation and discharge of fantasies cancels the energy wasted through repression. Its manifestations have a symbolic value, constituting a language and a form of expression.

Play is an activity where contact with reality is partially suppressed. The return and withdrawal component to that state of partial negation will turn it into a form of evasion of everyday reality. And this is what a lot of people say: "I want to switch off, evade my problems for a while; when I'm playing a game it's as if I forget everything". Fantasising is another psychic space where the tendency of the unconscious psychic processes is manifested in order to function with the pleasure principle, thus withdrawing from what causes displeasure, negating or getting away from reality. Substituting pleasure for the rule of reality isn't carried out in one go but over the course of psychic evolution. As long as there are nuclei of satisfaction in the body that serve as bridges to escape a situation of frustration, the same bridges that force the subject to establish the principle of reality, there will be sectors of the personality that will find refuge and protection in that mechanism.

Another way of understanding what happens in play is to visualise the space that is created in sport as a transitional area. There is a virtuality of time and space. What happens there is real, it's determined by a time-space boundary, but to a certain extent it remains suspended from exterior reality. As an instrument for obtaining pleasure and withdrawal over oneself, points of contact with what has been observed regarding the pleasure of movement are noted. Furthermore, the capacity for play can be considered as an achievement, a non-neurotic acquisition (Winnicott, 1971, pp. 47–52).

The socialisation that sport makes possible through play must also be stressed: the ludic aspect boosts communication. As a less involved way of relating to others, sport's expressive potential is greater than more "serious" types of interaction. That which is instinctive is also expressed through play. It would be worth asking how much sport is a sublimatory activity, or if we're talking about sport as an activity that can substitute other instinctive satisfactions.

Let us consider a known and questioned issue: before an important competition, trainers try to prevent their players from having sexual intercourse, arguing that they could diminish energy for the competition.

Others argue that it's not a question of energy but of "concentration". What is undoubtedly true is that after a highly intense competition there is not much energy left for sexual activity, at least immediately after the game. With respect to substitute formations, as we study the causation of neurotic symptoms we see that these replace the instinctive process itself, which has been modified by defence actions against the instincts. Where the substitution of satisfaction is linked to a reduction of tensions, another qualitative aspect of symbolic substitution would remain where an unconscious content is replaced by another following certain associative lines. Sport would allow us to account for the quantitative aspect as muscular discharge and the qualitative as game and competition, which, as such, allows for the display of implicated fantasies and their corresponding symbolic content.

We could also say that sport is a sublimatory activity, if we keep in mind that instead of directly satisfying sexual or aggressive instincts it alters their objectives in directing them towards objects or socially valued activities. Sporting activity implies a certain amount of sublimatory activity apart from substitute activity, as it transforms the content of direct sexual satisfaction into another content: beating the opponent as a symbolic substitute for "killing the father", for example. We should also keep in mind that sport is universalised and promoted as an ideal by vast sectors of the media.

Sport has a repetitive component but it also implicitly makes aesthetic creativity possible—rhythm, synchronisation, and even choreographic movements—which once again brings us closer to the idea of sublimation. It also contains the sublimation of aggression, since in the competition a socially accepted transformation of the death wish of the rival takes place. Based on a more radical conception, we notice that when there is a pure instinctive discharge, there is no play—it is interrupted. And vice versa, if there is play it's because there is no instinctive discharge. This instinctive discharge occurs in any sport when a doubt arises with respect to the legitimacy of a knock, kick, etc. or the validity of a goal or point scored (whether the ball hit the baseline, was in or out, or whether the player was offside or not).

In short, since sublimation is curtailed sexuality in its end and its object, is creative (it transforms nature of a non-instinctive character), produces pleasure, and is generally appreciated and not censured by society, sport activity could also be considered as a sublimatory activity.

In the following diagrams I summarise some of the concepts expressed so far: an alteration of both the internal and external reality is produced through play.

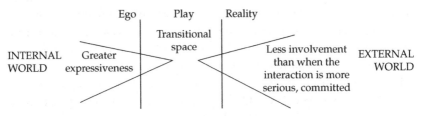

Diagram 1. Internal and external reality during play.

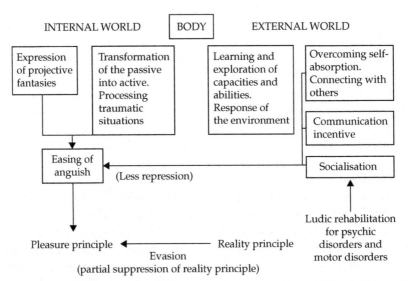

Diagram 2. The functions of play.

I shall now consider certain aspects of play in adults. Going over other conceptions of play, we can note that there are those that maintain that all culture originated from play: "play is older than culture, since as much as we like to stretch the concept of the latter, it always presupposes a human society and animals haven't waited for man to teach them how to play" (Huizinga, 1949, p. 1). If we consider an object used in play, the ball, we can see the fascination it exerts over any person at any age, particularly those who play or have played football, who feel the compulsive need to take part in impromptu games.

An elderly person, who sees a ball coming towards him in the park feels the irresistible need to hit it towards the children who are playing with it. The individual will feel that he has done something useful; and even an obscure and worn sense of belonging to a club of their youth ... The leadership of the ball is no accident. Its spherical shape relates it to one of humanity's oldest symbols through philosophers like Parmenides or poets like Rilke. The sphere represents the perfect form, the coincidence of the one and the whole, it's the image of the infinite. From ancient times, men have played with round forms, primitive and brutal games, as if they wanted to become familiar with that almost sacred object in those mysterious syntheses between war and celebration ... (Riviere, 2007, p. 229)

Types of play

We can distinguish four kinds of games, based on the variety of ludic impulses that all adults have (Caillois, 1958, pp. 11–37). One of these is the agonistic game, which is the one we observe in sport competitions in general; it is concerned with the compliance with rules, discipline, and perseverance. Second, Alea (a name attributed to a Greek soldier of the Trojan War who invented the dicing game Tabula) are games based on chance (roulette, cards, dice). This form of play, although not exclusively, is one that lends itself to all kinds of martingales. In competitive sport we also frequently witness invocation to all kinds of superstition on the part of players and spectators alike; for example, the items of clothing or good luck charms worn to win last year's championship, where the team stayed, or where and with whom the game was watched. This behaviour can also include consulting with modern day witches or necromancers when a certain team "has the jinx". We can see here traces of animist and magic thought, characteristic of children and our primitive ancestors. Here, natural phenomena is subjected to a person's will in order for them to protect themselves from enemies and all kinds of perilous situations and gives that person the power to harm those who are hostile or perceived as such. Its essence consists of substituting the laws of nature with laws of a psychological kind, or "mistaking an ideal relationship with a real one". That which drives the exercise of magic is nothing more than human desires (Freud, 1912–13, p. 84). Children as well as primitive peoples place an exaggerated value and great trust in the power of their desires. In adults, those who suffer from obsessive rationality load their mental processes so intensely that they end up assigning efficiency and validity only to that which has been intensely thought out. They reach the extreme of believing that any coincidence is a secondary matter. Through these considerations, we can shed light on the absurd and sometimes amusing practices that individuals resort to so that their team may win.

Another psychoanalytic perspective (Abadi, 1963, pp. 366–373) suggests that oracular interrogation carried out through chance corresponds to the equivalence life/death instead of winning/losing, which ultimately is a derivation of the anguish of death. We can relate these concepts to the anguish of castration (destiny that stamps its seal) or, additionally, the regressive experience of the fusional embrace of the Goddess of Fortune, equivalent to the archaic mother figure who gives life (luck) or kills (bad luck, jinx, bankruptcy).

Ilinx games—which include all those games of vertigo and those already described as passive or mixed forms of the pleasure of movement—and mimicry are two other categories within this classification. In the latter, the basis is linked with "looking like someone else", "being someone else". It is the principal game of children, where imitation has to do with identification with an ideal or admired character. Perhaps we could include in this category games like playing at being a king, a general, a captain, or a saviour.

The importance given to winning or losing games changes from amateur to professional sport, with the impact on a player's career being much more significant at top level. The resulting rewards or punishments, mainly economic, take the agonistic or competitive element of play to its maximum level. This approximates the situation to a battle where what is at stake is life (winning) or death (losing). Its dramatic quality is encouraged and appropriated by the media as a way of capturing the interest of the spectators. Few players can avoid this situation, but are compensated by being able to enjoy their gifts/talents—especially those who have the magic touch or "the lighted flame" of creativity and who stand out for the richness of their movements and manoeuvres. These players are the ones who enter the football pitch to play and enjoy themselves. They are the ones who make the dodges and the nutmegs—the magic football tricks that bring so much delight to spectators. In Argentina they are often compared to jugglers, magicians, or fine embroiderers.

These players, capable of preserving ludic pleasure, are the ones touched by the magic wand in any sport; technically gifted, yet also unyielding to the yoke of having to obtain results; the magical wrists in tennis, those who have "eyes in the back of their head" to pass or receive the ball, the fantastic cleats and studs on their boots or the exact and adequate field of vision. We see in these instances the opposition of routine, of what is mechanical and results-oriented, in favour of that which is improvised, creative, disruptive and entertaining. In this respect, great responsibility lies with the trainers and coaches, since it is up to them to nurture creativity and bring together tactical discipline with the necessary fireworks needed to win matches, finals, and championships.

Players who have undergone these experiences recognize and identify themselves with these qualities, incorporating them as a way of life. Waldo Kantor, well-known Argentine volleyball player and member of the National team for many years, made the following comment with respect to an athlete's retirement, letting transcend that "small flame" which has always beat and vibrated in all great players: "... one always remains a player, even after retirement from active competition. ..." Implicit in this is an aspect which has to do with personal and social identity (being recognized as a player) but which can also be observed in other artistic or professional fields. At this point, we assimilate the player to the artist. We find that both share a particular way of relating elements of their internal world, pouring them into the outside world (game, artwork). The game and the creative act become a kind of "as if", where reality gets blurred in its operating mode and contents and processes emerge that cross the barrier of repression more freely. By way of illustration, let's consider the following paragraphs, written about one of the greatest football players

... there is no way of foreseeing the pranks of this inventor of surprises never to be repeated and which he enjoys, perplexing computers. He's [Maradona] not a fast player, a little bull with short legs, but he carries the ball sewed to his legs and has eyes in all his body. His jugglery lights up the pitch. He can resolve a match by making a sudden and fatal kick with his back turned to the goal or making an impossible pass, from far away and surrounded by thousands of enemy legs; and there's no one to stop him when he launches himself forward, dodging opponents. (Galeano, 2000, p. 58)

The following reference regards another famous football star, Pele, "… as he ran, he passed through his rivals like a knife … he leaped as if the air were a ladder …" (ibid.).

I would like to conclude this chapter with an extract from the first interview between the sports journalist Horacio Pagani and Diego A. Maradona, taken from his book *El fútbol que le gusta a la gente* (Pagani, 2006, p. 71):

M: … I've been playing with a ball as long as I can remember …

P: … you started doing tricks with the ball …

M: … Not exactly. I used to reach the ball during the matches of Argentinos Juniors. During half-time, I started juggling with the ball because I wanted to. Since people began to enjoy it, it became a habit … I want to play, it's something that comes from inside …

P: How did you go in the summer tournament in the city of Mar del Plata?

M: I think I did OK, I made two goals and a "nutmeg".

P: What do you mean? You count every time you nutmeg?

M: In First Division yes, because I've had very few matches …

P: He's only 16 years old and has the frankness of an adolescent. His story is still a lad's adventure … it's an illusion, and Argentine football is in great need of illusions …

CHAPTER FOUR

Competition

The agonistic is the irreplaceable factor in sport. It derives from the Greek word *agón*, "struggle", and is the name given to competitive games in Greece. It has two aspects that must be considered: a) the discharge of aggression, and b) rivalry. The modes of manifesting aggression are closely related with the various ways of expressing the so-called mastery instinct. Above all, its support lies in the muscles. An antithetic activity/passivity pair exists that is mentally activated as a disjunction of dominating/being dominated.

Domination goes hand in hand with the externalisation of sadistic impulses. We can associate it with children and conducts of violence towards toys, animals, or other children. Its purpose isn't to make the other suffer but to be able to externalise that instinctive flow tainted with destructiveness and in this way deflect it outwards from the subject's own self. This instinctive mode will later influence sexual conduct; it will determine ways of acting and relating to others, which will manifest as the need for conquest. If we stop to observe what happens in sport during situations of confrontation, we'll see with what crudity and clarity styles and difficulties can manifest what has been mentioned above. When a game is played, tension and discharge are liberated, but the tendency to kill, destroy and dominate is also let loose. In order to win, a good share of sadism is also needed to release the "killer instinct". The channel for this is the muscles, often with the aid of a bat, a racket, or a ball.

The case of Leonor

Let's consider a clinical example. Leonor is a sixteen-year-old girl, the third of seven siblings. Like her mother, she started to play tennis when she was very young. Mother and daughter continue to play together until Leonor joins a school, betters her game, stands out as a player, and begins to train and participate in tournaments. The mother strongly encourages Leonor to dedicate herself to tennis, thus fulfilling one of her own long-time dreams. She takes Leonor to games, watches her train, and does everything possible to help her daughter continue along that career path.

The trainer suggests to Leonor that she should consult a psychologist, since she's technically very good but is afraid of winning. She can play to have fun, to let loose her tension, to socialise with friends, but the competition scenario and having to score points and win confronts her with a paradox: winning satisfies her mother's expectations in a relationship that resembles a trap. If Leonor wanted to place herself in a dominating position, adopting a more aggressive attitude, she would inexorably have to be recognised as someone different, separated; and this is where she gets stuck.

We know that "in order to assert herself and at the same time find a way of taking possession of objects, persons, situations (winning games), training herself in the use of power or control, she must previously fight to the death within the dual relationship (symbiosis mother-daughter) in order to achieve through this process her own recognition" (Del Valle Echegaray & Moise de Borgnia, 1996, p. 67). This struggle is enacted outside and avoided within the therapy relationship. Leonor preferred me to ask her questions rather than free associate, since nothing came out and her mind was blank. It was her way of not dealing with her own desires, erotic as well as aggressive.

Two years after she started therapy, she travelled abroad for three months to play tennis. On that occasion, she only manifested an intense phobia with regards to travelling by plane. A year later, and with the possibility of studying and playing in another country, where she would go by herself, she was able to make explicit her wish to be accompanied by her father. Leonor commented that she was no longer afraid of winning (the fight to the death with the mother); at this stage she was worried about losing or disappointing (her father). It is enlightening at this point to consider Fenichel: "fears and inhibitions in sport performance, prototypical situation of so many players, represent substitutes not only of the early bond with the mother figure, but also of the way of organizing the (oedipal) triangle" (1945, pp. 175–184).

In addition, given that those who struggle to express themselves verbally use body language instead, we started to create with Leonor a field of interpretation of all that had happened to her (she had few reflexive thoughts and regards about herself but sometimes she repeated to me what friends had observed about her) as a way of accessing her interior world. In one session, she remembered a friend's comment regarding how she was losing games ("you're stiff when you play, as if you are made of wood"). This allowed her to think and start to admit her ambivalence towards the trip abroad that she was about to undertake.

Rivalry

Moving on to the second aspect of competition or the agonistic game, which is the struggle with rivalry, the first rival is the father, who prohibits incest and prevents the satisfaction of the child's sexual desires with the mother. In Darwin's evolutionist model, taken up by Freud, its phylogenic origin goes back to the mythical father of the primitive horde, who possessed all the women and prevented the direct sexual satisfaction of the rest of the group. His assassination created a new problem, since the brothers that got together to kill him became rivals of each other. Giving up these desires led to the creation of a primitive social organisation, among whose rules of coexistence appeared the prohibition of incest.

Sport presents the possibility of "playing out rivalry". Winning would imply obtaining supremacy over others to satisfy sexual desire. The relationship with that totemic father was ambivalent. Not only was he hated, but he was also loved, and his assassination subsequently originated the feeling of guilt. A similar ambivalent bond is recreated in sport. Rivalry and fellowship frequently coexist among players. It is interesting to note as well that in all sports rivals are nearly always of the same sex.

Popular culture captures these unconscious contents very well. It is said that when one team or player repeatedly wins against another, a "paternity" takes place; the winner "adopts the loser as a son". It can also be argued that sport channels a certain degree of homosexual libido. One of its forms would be the pleasure produced by physical contact with competitors of the same sex, whether during the game or in the subsequent victory celebrations. Of course, the possibility of contact depends on the game, being greater in some cases (wrestling, football, rugby) or with certain objects serving as intermediaries (the net in tennis or volleyball, or on a more minimal scale, chess pieces in a game of chess).

Another form would be represented by the fantasies involved, where scoring a point would imply searching for a homosexual submission of the adversary by kicking the ball into the goal or shooting one into the basket of the rival team. This sense is frequently taken up by the refrains of the fans, particularly in football, which directly allude to sexual contents. The scoffing delivered to the sympathisers of the opposing team comes from the same source. It can also be surmised that behind the desire to kill one's rival is the erotic content of subjecting to him sexually. And all this could refer to players as well as spectators, who, through an identifying mechanism, channel their own amount of desire.

Continuing with this analysis, we can add to the oedipal rivalry two other rivalries: between siblings, the brother/sister complex, and between friends and others, the neighbour complex. The brother or sister can be a rival or an ally. He or she can help us to loosen our dependency on our parents or can reinforce it (Kancyper, 1998, pp. 241–246; Landolfi, 1998, pp. 177–192). In other cases, the sibling can assume the mode of a double, the mirror image or the ideal.

The first murder that we find in the Bible is that of Abel by his brother Cain. Later on we find the saga of Joseph and his brothers. The brother is in fact the "first neighbour". He is that "unbearable other" who is the same but external to oneself, the "redundant" one who threatens our oneness. This sole-person fantasy tries to deny, in the psychic and material realities, the inescapable and structural fraternal confrontation (rivalry) (Kancyper, 1998, pp. 242–246).

From a different perspective, our neighbour is perceived as a threat to the illusory perfection of being, and for this reason he or she must be eliminated. Moreover the rival (intruder) is he who threatens the legitimacy of another's rights and at the same time re-signifies the concept of "homo hominis lupus" (a man is a wolf to another man) that underlies psychic life. This "lupus" (wolf) will be the one who has to come out onto the field to confront his opponent(s). The inability to do so or a preference to get away will demonstrate a lack of resolution in this neighbour complex, which will result in severe inhibitory effects, whether during the game itself or in other spheres of life. We need to explore this aspect in players when they comment on their lack of motivation or desire to compete, when the anguish or pressure in defining moments becomes excessively intense, and when comments like "I don't know what's happening to me; I want to know, but I don't understand" come to light.

We also need to consider the perspective of the other as non-equal, based on differences like regions, neighbourhoods and clubs, to aspects like religion and skin colour; such factors can be inexhaustible sources of hostile feelings, resulting in discrimination towards another and, in extreme cases, even homicide. From this perspective, the subject will try to make "the other" disappear or convince themselves that they are useless in order to reinforce the self-illusion, or that of his peers, of being the best. There would only be room for one person to be recognised as the ideal, the perfect one: the winner. The media actively participate in the collective imagination in referring to the successful player or goal scorer as a "killer", "warrior", "gladiator", "titan" or in associating him with military figures: "great captain", "marshal", or "commander".

The case of Stephen

Let's analyse another clinical situation. Steve is the fifth of thirteen siblings. From a humble background, he's the only one who has managed to succeed in sports, which has resulted in economic stability. He plays for a first division football club. Nevertheless, at a key moment of his career (being called to the national team), Steve develops a tendency to injure himself. He seeks a therapy consultation by his own initiative. He aspires to better himself, to improve; nevertheless, during the last six months he has suffered one injury after another. In his own words: "I live one thousand miles an hour".

Steve represents for his father and siblings the benefactor to whom they resort not only for financial support but emotional support, as counsellor and even arbitrator of their quarrels. All this is very gratifying for him, but also burdensome. He is torn between taking more care of himself, his wife and children and attending to the problems of his birth family. His feeling of guilt is intense, but at the same time denied. In that tug of war, injuries represent a possible transaction that can put a limit to the omnipotent and cannibalistic situation in which he finds himself. On the other hand, it's not easy for him to give up being a hero.

We observe that these different modes of agonism—oedipal rivalry, fraternity complex, and neighbour complex—are activated and generate effects or are articulated each time a game is played. It's much more intense for professional players, who are more distant from what is purely ludic and recreational. We will now delve into what is known as the fighting spirit. Biologically, it has been associated with levels of testosterone. In the field of sport psychology, it has been referred to as competitive aggression and it's an area that has been explored in order to maintain performance and results for players and teams. It is closely related to the motivation and readiness felt before a sporting event.

Many trainers appeal to manipulation and suggestion. Their main objective is to mobilise the psychic layers of players, creating atmospheres and experiences that make them want to give their all. This is achieved by combining images (films and photos of epic deeds) with sounds (melodies, hymns, words of relatives). At times, trainers request visits from significant figures from the club (president, ex-players), from sport (national idols), or from the nation (ministers, presidents) in order to boost these effects. The aim of this is to create heroic figures—great individuals that will be admired by their fellow human beings. This represents, both for individual and collective psychology, the desired goal in order to satisfy family and social ideals and obtain ultimate love, respect, and admiration. Those springs of emotion and sentiment are enhanced by the atmosphere of the group, by the "us", by the "all for one and one for all", in that mystique that promotes the fusion of individuals into one body, represented by the group, the team, the national T-shirt.

These manoeuvres have as an antecedent the warmongering diatribes that commanders used to give to their soldiers before battle. The secret of their effectiveness lies in knowing what will stir a particular group. And they have as a support the influence that the trainer has in the minds of each and every one of the players as their leader; he is the custodian of the ideal of all the others, and fans will put the players on a pedestal thanks to his leadership.

In the next section, let's take as an example what occurred during the final of the European Cup in 2009 between Manchester United and Barcelona, as well as the final of the Libertadores de America Cup during the same year between Cruzeiro (Brazil) and Estudiantes de la Plata (Argentina).

Motivating videos for players

An article published in *La Nación* newspaper (2009) describes how coaches are increasingly keeping in mind messages that are emotionally appealing to players in order to help their game. Diego Maradona did it with poster boards in the changing rooms of the Argentine National Team. And Pep Guardiola showed a video of players intermingled with scenes from the film *Gladiator* before the final of the Champions League in Barcelona. The Estudiantes players didn't want to give many details about the hours preceding the game with Cruzeiro, but it transpired that Alejandro Sabella had shown them videos with messages from their relatives. It is also known that the images were filmed throughout the Libertadores Cup.

The team from La Plata also found impetus in the triumphal mood that took over the Brazilians after the 0-0 draw in La Plata. In the changing rooms of the visiting team, a fan was displayed showing the Libertadores Cup 2009 as having already been won by Cruzeiro. Scarves had also been made celebrating the assured victory of the home team.

The video that helped Barcelona win the champions league

On 2 June 2009, *Clarín* published an article about Pep Guardiola and the video that he had shown to his team. Less than a week after Barcelona's conquest of the Champions League in Rome, TV3 Channel aired the video, which was shown to the team before the final with Manchester United. "I need a favor to be able to win the European Cup", was the text message from coach Guardiola to Santi Pedró, a friend of his. The only request was that the entire squad appear on the video. It lasted seven minutes and featured all the players, from Victor Valdés to Lionel Messi, intermingled with scenes from the film *Gladiator*. The film is set in Rome, which is also where the final was played at the Olímpico. "Nessun dorma" was the soundtrack. It was apparently seen by the Barca team at 20:28, just seventeen minutes before the defining game.

According to the Spanish media, the combination of images with the music of "Turandot" by Puccini deeply moved the players in the darkness of the changing room in Rome.

Writers, in describing sporting events, often resort to metaphors of war. This can be appreciated in the following excerpts from Eduardo Galeano's *Football in Sun and Shadow*:

> In football, ritual sublimation of war, eleven men in shorts become the sword of the neighborhood, city or nation. These warriors without arms or armor exorcize the devils of the multitude, confirming their faith: in each confrontation between two teams, ancient hatreds and loves, inherited from parents to children, engage in combat.
>
> The stadium has towers and standards, like a castle, and a deep wide moat around the field. In the middle, a white line indicates the territories in dispute. At each end, the goals await, which will be bombarded by football hits. The area just in front of the goals is referred to as danger zone.
>
> In the central circle, the captains exchange flags and greet each other as the ritual demands. The referee blows the whistle and the ball, another wind that whistles, is set in motion. As the ball comes and goes, a player gains control and "strolls" with it until he receives a fatal kick, falling helplessly to the ground. The victim doesn't get up. In the vastness of the green pitch, he lies. In the immensity of the stands, voices thunder, as enemy fans graciously roar: "Let him die"…
>
> By means of a clever tactical manoeuvre of the foreseen strategy, our squadron charged, surprising the unsuspecting rival. It was a devastating attack. When the local hosts invaded enemy territory, our battering ram opened a breach on the most vulnerable flank of the defensive wall and infiltrated itself towards the danger zone. The gunner received the missile, skillfully placed himself in firing position, prepared the finish and culminated the offensive by firing the cannon-shot that annihilated the cancerberus. Then, the defeated guardian, custodian of the bastion that seemed impenetrable, fell on his knees with his face between his hands as the executioner raised his hands before the cheering multitude …
> (2000, p. 18)

We now need to consider competition from a psychological perspective. The analysis of persons with strong competitive traits makes it possible to observe that they displace from their internal world situations of fear or anxiety that are difficult to manage at the intra-psychic level. An attitude of defiance is a characteristic trait frequently found in these individuals. Moreover Deutsch observed that "… when they located those challenges in forces of nature (mountains, air, water) through adventures, in establishing limits (time, distances) or in rivals (persons) they needed to overcome, they were able to liberate themselves to a large extent, finding relief from such anxieties and fears" (1926, pp. 223–227).

Internal conflicts can occur from the collision between different desires or aspirations. This can result in anxiety and inhibition, and the feeling of a loss of potential and ability. On the other hand, if the situation is confronted externally, a person will be able to evaluate its strengths and weaknesses. In short, a person will be able to make a general analysis of the situation. This process will provide a test or measure of their abilities, which in turn will be a source of personal satisfaction. They are also permitted and socially validated actions, just as displays of strength or the use of violence and aggression are, in order to win. It is noteworthy that in taking on external, competitive, and sporting challenges "… a painful internal experience is subverted by one of well-being, success and power" (ibid., pp. 223–227). The current competitive culture, with its strong phallocentric overtones, makes it easier for many men and women in our society to turn sport into a custom and even a ritualised way of life (particularly during weekends).

CHAPTER FIVE

Transference

The notion of transference, developed in *The Dynamics of Transference* (Freud, 1912b, pp. 99–108), is a phenomenon that not only appears during psychoanalytic treatment but also in daily life and is characterised by being of an unconscious nature.

The instinctive and erotic tendencies of each individual originate from the joint action of a person's congenital disposition and childhood experiences as well as the influx of later impressions. This results in a kind of cliché or behavioural pattern that is repeated and reproduced throughout a lifetime. Since some of our erotic and emotional needs are not satisfied in reality, their development is arrested. Nevertheless, they might unfold in the life of fantasy, remaining confined in our unconscious. Normally, some of these tendencies manage to achieve a complete psychic evolution, while the part that remained postponed, in a state of regression, will try to satisfy or discharge itself in any new person that appears on the horizon.

Since this pattern or disposition is related to persons who have been involved in the subject's history, what will be transferred will be related to the father, mother, brother, or other significant figure from childhood. In order for this to take place there must be something within the unconscious complex that lends itself to being transferred, which "fits" with the person to whom the transference is directed. For this reason, we can affirm that transference is a kind of relationship that brings with it feelings towards someone that are inappropriate, since they really involve someone else. The subject reacts with a person from his present as if he or she were someone from his past; it's a repetition or reissue of a former tie.

As an unconscious phenomenon, the person doesn't realise that his feelings, desires, fears, fantasies, attitudes, ideas or defences are impregnated with inappropriate nuances. Nevertheless, there is a mixture of reactions in all the relationships or ties that are established, with only one part remaining tainted by the transference phenomenon. All other aspects of the personality will have had a more complete psychic evolution, and therefore will be more discriminating and conforming to realistic standards or objectives with respect to the characteristics of the person with whom the subject relates with.

If we try to particularise or differentiate the more realistic aspects from the more regressive or archaic, we find qualities that enable us to identify them. The reactions where transference predominates are always inappropriate, due to the quality, quantity or duration of the reaction. In addition, they are usually more tenacious, obstinately capricious, and strongly ambivalent. When all these characteristics appear, we can affirm that the pattern of emotional and erotic disposition that originated in childhood has been displaced to a given figure or person.

In the sport world, this happens very frequently and is due to several factors. At the beginning of their career, many athletes are children or adolescents; relationships are established as the result of having to spend many hours together. Very close affective, economic and professional dependencies are forged. This combination favours the production of regressive (child-like) patterns and consequently the displacement and installation of intense transferences. As a result, and due to the effect of the unconscious, the individual attributes, just as in dreams, actuality and reality to the result of his unconscious impulses, inciting his passions without taking into account the real situation.

We also observe that, due to the transference, there exists an influx exercised by the mechanism of suggestion. This can be studied when we review the effects of hypnosis and confirm that suggestion is established as a nucleus of the hypnosis. Suggestion is defined "... as a representation or conscious idea instilled in the brain of the hypnotized person by an external influence and accepted by that person as if it had spontaneously emerged ..." and "... it's possible to distinguish it from other forms of psychic influx like the order, communication or instruction because in its case a representation awakens in someone else's brain which is not examined in respect of its origin but which is spontaneously accepted as if it had naturally emerged in that brain ..." (Freud, 1888–89, p. 82).

Auto-suggestions also exist, which are like inductions generated unconsciously by the subject himself. They deserve our attention, since we can observe that many of the experiences that players, athletes and teams go through are founded on this nucleus. Suggestion acts in such a way as to make the subject believe and feel confidence, support and security, sentiments that are necessary for any athlete. This belief and suggestion can operate almost magically by means of a look, a presence, a gesture, or a word. In addition, they can obtain (suggestive) effects that make the athlete want to go on, fight, try harder, not give up, and believe more in himself and his potential. In groups or teams, these beliefs have an influence in the creation of a mystique, a force that allows them to achieve stardom, that injects in them bravery, energy, and sufficiency.

Let's consider the following example. Osvaldo Suarez, a glorious figure in Argentine athletics, several times winner of the Saint Sylvester Race, and Olympic marathon runner, used to say:

> There is a moment during the race when one feels that pain and exhaustion take hold of one's legs, you're left without air and think that it's impossible to go on. At that moment the most important thing is to keep one's head. I had faith in myself; I knew that they couldn't defeat me. Also, the presence of persons that encourage one, give one confidence, like my trainer Alejandro Stirling, was very helpful. I was able to listen and distinguish his cry amongst thousands of people. The suggestive effect of words and sometimes the exchange of glances with a trainer at that difficult moment of the race had the effect of necessary protection and confidence that made me feel what I had often heard, repeated and evoked: "I know you can do it", "you're going to win", "you're the best". (Personal communication)

All this had a stimulating effect that allowed him to overcome the barrier of exhaustion and pain to reach the finish line.

Another example is provided by Juan Carlos Menseguez, a forward for San Lorenzo de Almagro. During a match against River Plate in the 2007/2008 tournament, he felt his legs weighing on him and found it difficult to run and with little confidence. His performance during the first half had not been satisfactory. Soon after the second half had started, he heard the coach of the rival team tell one of the defensive players to team up with another so that they could both mark him. Juan Carlos said that the effect of those words "loosened" him; he started to improve his game, had goal opportunities, and didn't feel that previous weight on his legs.

What happened psychologically? Evidently there was a suggestive influx. The voice of the coach of the rival team alerting his own players with respect to the danger he represented as something real and tangible made him feel and believe himself more dangerous and capable; this allowed him to loosen up and set himself free from the weight that obstructed him. This influx, in turn, was added to the confidence already instilled by his own coach when he placed him in the starting line-up, together with his own wish (desire) to play better.

In another example of suggestive influx, athlete Andrew Osagie revealed in an interview with the *Guardian* newspaper (Kessel, 2012) how a meeting with Olympic gold medallist Steve Ovett helped fuel his ambition to achieve glory in London. The twenty-four year old from Harlow met Ovett, the 800 m champion in 1980, in New York. "That for me was a big positive, him saying to me: 'You've got something, keep going, you've got something,'" said Osagie. "That was really good, it was inspirational and it will definitely spur me on for these last five weeks … Those few words meant more than sitting down for an hour with a coach; this was someone who's been there and done it."

Why do we review transferences?

As I have already mentioned, transferences comprise the spectrum of ties and relationships that permanently impacts on events in the life and career of an athlete. In fact, motivation, concentration or dispersion during certain periods or moments of a match has its origin in transferences. It is therefore important to detect transferences, since this will help to modify dispositions and conduct that which will benefit the mental health of the athlete. On occasions, we can intervene directly, interpreting in the here and now; in other instances, by clarifying or pointing out the way in which those ways of reacting or feeling generate responses in others.

Transference with the trainer

The trainer generally occupies the place of group leader or paternal substitute, which can result in associating or repeating aspects of the tie that the subject had or would have liked to have had with the father or other figures of authority. Intense feelings of ambivalence are frequently observed as well as the search for protection, advice, and doing or not doing things in order to be loved/approved by him with the subsequent expectations of reward, love, and acceptance. On the other hand, disillusionments and disappointments can reach the extreme of motivating ruptures and are generally influenced by these ambivalent feelings.

The difficult task is to distinguish between the personal and professional tie. Moreover, with regards to the phenomenon of transference we must consider the reality of trainers as mentors and guides; young athletes, often having migrated from distant places, find themselves in new environments, now having to spend many hours with trainers, assistants, or managers. The trainer can be father, guide, tutor, and teacher. He provides conduct guidelines; how to dress, how to invest one's earnings, advice on acquaintances (especially with regards to distinguishing people that are genuine from those with ulterior motives), and health recommendations. At football clubs, there are other figures that can take charge, such as the coaches, who will come to establish a bond of confidence and companionship, which, added to suggestion and affinities, results in mentoring.

Trainers are also in need of therapy in order to detach themselves from this direct paternal role and maintain the appropriate distance that their position demands. Whether they shorten the distance too much or whether they stretch it, this will bring as a consequence emotional responses from the players, especially those with more infantile traits, who demand attention and affection. The task that they carry out as part of their job must be supplemented by the assistance of a professional that can shed some light on these emotional labyrinths. Osvaldo Suarez used to say: "… the trainer is very important. He made me believe that nobody could defeat me. I was very resolved and determined and I also exercised mental discipline. I had faith in myself that I was going to win.

The psychologist serves to give confidence and mental power to the athlete" (personal communication).

Luis Lobo, a former tennis player, commented that as a trainer his players, when facing an opponent with a strong serve, would ask him with regard to each serve where they should stand to receive the ball; whether at the T, angled to the right, etc. Obviously, Luis couldn't predict what would happen any more than the players could. Nevertheless, the fact that he took on that responsibility of telling tennis players what to do fostered confidence and gave them peace of mind and assurance. This illustrates the strength of transference in a figure of knowledge and authority, and a strong suggestive impact.

Transference with the public (the fans)

With their applause or booing, and with their insults or encouraging cries, fans can be placed in the role of judge or a god to whom victory is offered. For this reason, they always have an impact, particularly at a home game: the presence of an audience always exercises an effect on the mind of the player. Frequently, the encouragement on the part of the crowd (cries, choruses, chants) serves to emotionally stimulate players, managing in this way to increase performance. The players make a greater effort, playing until their last drop of sweat, as the saying goes. It's for this reason that many teams win more frequently when they are "on their own turf".

Fans can boost the emergence of an oceanic feeling, resembling that which is mystical or religious. Such a feeling is similar to an experience that is limitless or has no barriers; it's a kind of blending with others, a communion with the whole. In Freud's words "This experience would appear by a regression to a primitive or early state of the sense of self. Originally, the ego includes everything, later beginning to loosen from itself an exterior world. Our present sense of ego is none other than the atrophied residue of a wider feeling … that corresponded to a more intimate communion between the ego and the world around it. This primary sense of ego subsists in the emotional life of many human beings, set against an adult's sense of ego, whose limits are more precise and constrained" (Freud, 1930a, p. 66).

The feeling of selfhood begins to be formed at the breastfeeding stage, when we begin to discern between self and others, interior and exterior, ego and non-ego. In order for this to occur, the experiences of pleasure/displeasure become necessary, as do the contrasts between reality and fantasy. Other factors will also be added to these experiences, like the processes of identification and the various development crises. In pathological scenarios, a loss of feeling about self or states of mental confusion can be observed. During adult life, there are states like falling in love where the feeling of fusion with the other, being two in one, is also experienced.

I suggest that fans provoke something similar in the players, in making them feel as one with the crowd. It's as if the fans are protective parents, the ones who are always there for a team or a sports star, regardless of the circumstances. Comments like "I'll follow you wherever you go", "if you lose, I don't give a damn", and "I've been a fan since birth ..." give an idea of the unconditional love that has its roots in primary and longed-for ways of relating to others. Fans invite players to connect with them; they know that in this way it will lessen their inhibitions, enabling a sports star to display his or her full potential.

Tennis also provides examples that show how the communion with fans serves to influence the mood, motivation, and level of performance of players. We only need to remember "The wave that saved Gaudio" article (Devries, 2004), after the final he won at Roland Garrós:

> ... When Gaudio got ready to serve 3/4 the "wave" appears. The particular way European spectators have of expressing themselves by progressively standing up from their seats throughout the stadium in order to provoke a movement similar to that of a wave. For those of us who were present, it seemed clear that the public spontaneously looked for its own way of seeking enjoyment in the advent of that Final's frustrating epilogue. The wave prolonged itself for several minutes, leaving the game in suspense. Both players were surprised. Coria seemed upset by the delay. Gaudio, who looked towards the top stand (perhaps for the first time during the game), placed his racket on the court floor and started to clap at the collective spectacle. He then relaxed. And "another Gaudio appeared". His game began to loosen up and he won his serve, leaving Coria with zero. When the score reached 4/4, a feminine voice was heard from the top stand yelling "Gaudio, I love you very much", in a Spanish with a French accent. Smiles from the stadium and greetings from Gaudio to that unexpected display of feelings. His hits improved, and he won the set 6/4.

Gaudio declared in a French newspaper that the wave was the key to his change: "In fact, that's true. That social expression made his change easier, a shift in his position. A psychic positioning from somewhere else inside him. That public, possibly represented internally up to that moment with dark colors and sanctioning terms, afterwards probably in brighter colors, accompanied him in his new place. One of self-confidence, of pleasurable feelings that stimulated precisely the dramatic micro-orders which trigger the best decisions, the more precise hits, the least amount of errors, the greater capacity...".

But there are also fans that devour, that are hungry for success at any price, and that become brutal and denigrating when their expectations are not met. Whilst the rejection of players by the fans is an influence that could never be totally ignored, the technical staff are generally more "sensitive" towards players and will not necessarily act on fans' demands; for example, in cases where they are demanding the substitution of a player. If a defeat is suffered that is particularly humiliating, the abuse from fans can be followed by pressure in the changing room and in the media.

For all this illusory support, many players are responsible for "working the realistic tie" with the fans in order to gain personal benefit. This can include statements designed for media effect ("I dedicate it to all these people who have supported us, which is what matters"), since that illusory element will later have an effect on the chants, and boost encouragement and positive presence. Players learn that a "palate" exists that varies according to each team and determines the taste for certain characteristics of the game (for example, being more dedicated, marking the opponents more, being more committed, doing more tricks with the ball, dodging and weaving with greater aesthetic display and ability). Those who have played for various clubs often change their style in order to receive the applause of fans (this is evident in a skilful player who adds pressure, blocks the game of his opponent and pursues his rivals—all these actions being synonymous with strength and courage). Some fans are famous for their "dark palate", an allusion to their high technical expectations with respect to their team.

Players may provoke rival fans, making moves to upset them, in order to motivate their own game. This is none other than a manipulation by which the player, conscious of that which he knows will help his game, searches for the cries of fans in order to engage more with the game and perform better.

Transference with the rival

In referring to competition and rivalry, at least three areas of possible meaning were identified: the fraternal, the oedipal, and the neighbour. Let's analyse an example: on the occasion of the Davis Cup between Argentina and the USA in 1992, interviews with the Argentine players were held before the game. One of them stated that he was going to play against an idol whom he had never confronted. After Argentina comfortably won the first set, their performance started to decline dramatically and inexplicably; innumerable mistakes were made until the game was finally lost.

We can infer that the idol in question was located in the child imago of the paternal place (idol, ideal), in the mind of the player. Winning implied dethroning that father figure, with all the cortege of retaliation and subsequent guilt. When the moment of the game arrived where victory was about to become a reality (I insist that this is a possible theoretical hypothesis), the mistakes and subsequent defeat placed father (unattainable idol) and son in their respective places. For this reason, it's always important to be aware of the influence that any rival may have, since it can intimidate or oppress the player, sometimes consciously, but often unconsciously. Likewise, underestimating a rival can lead to inattentions that can result in surprises and the loss of matches.

In another example, a professional tennis player comments that when he has to confront players he hates, he freely lets out all his competitive aggression; however, when he feels friendlier towards an opponent, he feels sorry for them or perceives him as inferior and it becomes impossible to win. Analysing his problem in more depth, we find out that he has a disabled brother whom he has always helped and loves very much. We suppose that when he confronts an equal (brother), this aspect of the unconscious fraternal complex is reactivated and, as a result, prevents him from discharging the aggressiveness necessary to win.

Where the "other" (neighbour complex) is the rival who must be eliminated, there are no approximations and there is no sport fellowship; only a persecutory feeling towards all. A player who is very marked by this complex doesn't make friends or integrate well in team sports. In this regard, a player who might supplant him in his own team is just as much of a rival as a player from another team. This feeling is also nourished by the player's reinforcement of small differences between himself and others in order to highlight his own identity by opposition.

It's necessary to talk before a game about rivals in order to clarify who they are and what skills and advantages they have—what they are able to do. In this way, the player is liberated from a possible transference trap. The trainer's task must be to show the technical and tactical characteristics of each opponent, thus enabling the player to confront them with a good chance of success. If the rival is known, an imprint may already exist that "fits" a referential pattern of transference; therefore a trainer can attempt to resolve it with all the resources previously mentioned.

Transference with the football agent

In recent times the football agent has increased his validity, assuming a more visible role in what concerns the life of the player. Nearly all the players of a first division team in Argentina have an agent, often from the early stages of their careers. These agents provide them with money, transport allowance, and contacts with influential people. They can also give their opinion regarding the professionals who assist the player (doctor, psychologist, nutritionist, physical therapist). The way of accessing an agent is either through a relative, club colleague, or a member of the institution the player belongs to. For some players, the agent is a family member.

The football agent is the person who obtains the contracts, prizes, and tournaments; he becomes a figure of power who can make important decisions regarding the economic aspects of the player's life. As mentioned, many athletes must migrate at an early age from their homes and live away from their parents. For this reason, agents, like managers/trainers, often become substitute parents. At times, they can come into conflict with the coach, the family or the institution linked to the player. The resulting dependency of the player on his agent increases the possibility of creating relationships of subjugation.

It would be helpful to include interviews with agents in order to broaden the complex web of factors that affect the players' psyche and performance, influencing, as well, their aspirations and frustrations.

However, this is a difficult area to address, particularly due to the economic and power issues involved. In this regard, the rule of money can
be directly linked to Freud's observation that "… as far as money is
concerned, people behave with the same hypocrisy, bashfulness and
secrecy that they employ when dealing with sexual matters" (1913c).
For this reason, it is no surprise that my attempt to approach this subject
generated endless resistances, so many in fact that they endangered the
exercise of my professional role.

Therapeutic approach

I stress that it is fundamental to make explicit to all members of technical staffs, relatives and participants that transference factors exist and
have an influence on all players and teams. We must always be aware
of its effect and the different ways in which transference presents itself
(jokes, ironies, moods, variations in performance) to be ready to work
with this phenomenon. Clarification through the signalling and subsequent interpretation of transference reactions is an essential aspect
of this work. The various ways of relating, real or imaginary, that are
present in the mind of the player as dispositions or attitudes will eventually have an impact on his motivation.

The transference link with the coach or the trainer must be worked
procedurally. That is, it's not simply a specific or occasional bond but
rather a continuous flow that needs to be clarified from distortions,
since it can easily fall into traps by way of anger or misunderstandings.
Therefore, during or before a match, it is important to elucidate the
issues that players have with rivals. Working with young players of a
football team, I was asked to check on their mood before a game against
a well-known rival, since there was a general feeling that they were
facing a defeat. Chatting with the group, certain information transpired, like having lost against that team during the previous round, the
physical stature of their opponents perceived as greater, and the fear
that in controversial situations the opponents would override them.
Regardless of the objective value of this information, I understood that
the belief in a "paternity" on the part of the rivals had been established.
This made the boys feel that they were in a position of weakness, which
would probably result in defeat.

After bringing this general belief out into the open, with its resulting
unconscious effect of what might happen during the game, I proposed

reviewing what they considered to be their own attributes as a team. The answer regarding their technical qualities was almost unanimous (skill, touch, circulation). Together with the coach, we reinforced (suggestion plus transference) the worth and forcefulness of their playing abilities. Through this mechanism, we managed to have an impact on the mood and belief of the group, providing support and greater assurance, elements that could offset the physical difference of their rivals. I must add that I provided some support during half-time as well. The final result of the game was a draw, which suggests that with the aid of psychological intervention, the mood, belief and performance of a team can be positively modified.

CHAPTER SIX

Pressures

Feeling pressure is a common experience in many situations of our lives, but its effect is especially noticeable in sport practices, particularly during high competition. It can be said that all athletes have experienced or suffered this sensation many times throughout their career. We could define pressure in sport as an experience that is normally expressed by a sensation of weight or tension that can manifest itself at the psychic or motor level. At the mental level, it consists of a distressing sensation or the perception that something is confronting the subject, an obstacle that must be overcome; this provokes a state of charge. It can turn into a discomfort (like worry), occupying more psychic space. The experience can be compared to sitting for an exam. These circumstances will demonstrate the aptitude of a player.

Once the competition starts, the player's own capacities and skills are set in motion. Performing at a level that is expected has a favourable effect on the player that facilitates relaxation. On the other hand, a poor performance, inferior to what is expected, or a very good performance on the part of the opponent, makes the tension rise.

Let's take as an example Emmanuel Ginóbili's declarations after the Argentine National Basketball Team lost their debut against Lithuania during the Olympic Games in Beijing 2008:

> On the other side, in the midst of sullen gestures and a certain degree of worry, strong words by Emanuel Ginóbili could be heard: "It's the first time we lose in the debut of a tournament". Later he added: "We made many mistakes, we were very tied up, perhaps due to the nerves of the debut and they made many triple shots. Sure I'm hurt; I hope that the defeat won't hit us too hard. Now we have more pressure than before. Losing during the last shot is even worse." In any case, his optimism appeared as always. "Now we must recover, the tournament doesn't end here, we still have time. We must try to forget this, quickly overcome this moment, and focus on Australia". (*La Nación*, 2008a)

At the motor level, what we usually find is a dystonia in the arousal process. In normal physiological conditions there is an adrenergic discharge when activation starts, with constriction of blood vessels and a synchronic rise of muscular tone. The dystonia implies that, due to the effects of the psychogenic stimulus (charge, tension) in the central nervous system, muscular groups activate themselves, but some of them will be hypotonic and others hypertonic.

Feeling tied-up (inhibition) is more frequent and, to a lesser degree, we observe an excess or acceleration, with a predominance of adrenergic tone. This state makes it difficult to adequately confront performance and prevent the rise of cramps, torn muscles, and more serious injuries, which lead to mistakes during the game. Motor dystonia can be the only visible manifestation that a player is undergoing a state of pressure. The simple observation of these states can alert us to the fact that something is also happening at the mental level, so that we can examine it and later treat it at the psychological level.

To sum up, pressure is a mental or body charge, a burden that weighs on the player; something that he must get rid of in order to feel free and unrestricted in the exercise of his skills. Pressure will always exert its influence, determining how loosened or constrained the player will be to confront the demands of each competition.

In order to better understand how we deal internally with pressure, it's necessary to describe the way in which the psychic apparatus, considered from a structural model, functions with instances that are sometimes articulated and sometimes in opposition to each other, generating tensions, conflicts, and internal struggles.

One part of the psychic apparatus will seek to manifest or discharge that which is purely instinctive. Another sector will be responsible for asserting the moral imperatives, the mandates and ideals that have gradually internalised themselves throughout the subject's development. It will stimulate pressure so that certain choices and desires may freely manifest themselves while others may not. Finally, a third sector will have to face the tug-of-war between the other two as well as the demands and conditions imposed by external reality in order for desires to materialise. In this sector lies the notion of self or ego (identity), the measure of one's own worth, and the functions that establish what must be done first—what must be postponed according to external circumstances and what course is convenient undertake. This part of the psychic apparatus might be more developed and have more strength and capacity to undertake its functions. We may refer then to either the strength of the ego or an ego that remains "captive of the servitudes" (Freud, 1923b, p. 56) imposed by internal or external instances; it will be more inhibited and incapacitated, and give in more to demands—we are referring, in this case, to a weak ego.

We can measure the development of the ego and its strength by its capacity to control and regulate impulses in demanding situations (competitions). If the ego found itself pulled in several directions at a certain moment (family or love conflicts, loyalties, guilt), it could find itself overwhelmed, manifesting as aggression, irritability, or low performance.

Some reactions or incomprehensible situations experienced by athletes can perhaps be explained if we analyse in more detail their internal and external causes. How can we explain, for example, the unexpected reaction of Zinedine Zidane, the French football star and captain of the French national team, to a provocation made by an opponent, Materazzi, in the World Cup final (2006) against Italy, having won the Ballon d'Or (Golden Ball) and playing his farewell game? What passed through his head? Where did so many years of experience, leadership and football wisdom end up? How can it be that he wasn't able to avoid the provocation, reacting as if he were in a street fight? It can be surmised that a series of factors (pain of leaving? family situations? being the best player of the World Cup? or other unconscious situations) could have combined in his brain to overwhelm him, making it impossible to control his reaction, which resulted in his uncalled-for response. The actual reason for Zidane's aggression and the subsequent expulsion from the pitch was not known until four years afterwards.

Many people blamed him for the French defeat in the final, but nobody cared to analyse the details of the situation. Zidane declared to the press in February 2010 that his mother was ill, and that the insult he received alluded to his mother. We may surmise that in his psyche situations of pain and mourning (the end of his sporting career, mother in a life-threatening situation) took over his emotions. The incident could have been the straw that broke the camel's back, making him react with violence. It's also evident that his lack of control was caused by a fault in the regulating mechanism. This speaks to us of pressure, and the ego measuring and regulating it as if it were a "pressure-ometer". Analysing the intimacy of these processes will provide answers unexplored until now, in this case as well as in many others.

In the following diagram, I illustrate the different pressures that can act on the mind and body of an athlete:

		Ideals	Ideal of Ego
PRESSURES	INTERNAL	Own expectations	Wishes Ambitions
		Self-commitment	Need to improve oneself
			Need for self-assertion
	PERSONAL EXTERNAL	Trainer	
		Other team members	
		Family	Parents, siblings, spouse
		Friends	
		Fans	Club, neighbourhood, city, country
		Media	
	CONTEXTUAL EXTERNAL	For the salary at stake	
		For the importance of the event	If they qualify for something major
			If they are relegated or lose points

Internal component

The internal component is strongly determined by imaginary factors. It will be motorised by the desires and ambitions that beat in the interior of the player: his hunger, his need. Each player knows how much he can give. From there, he will evaluate and compare his performance in relation to the ideal he would hope to have, to which he must add the viewpoint of those whose opinions are significant to him. The evaluation process can base itself in objective data or be distorted by an excess of expectations or an emotional state that enlarges or diminishes what he does or obtains. The sensation of pressure will also be proportional to the proximity of the ideal that is internally established.

An excess of self-commitment can lead to a state of brooding that can affect a player during a competition. This happened to Albert, a twenty-two-year-old professional football player who was considered a "cold" or unemotional player. He didn't seem to be affected by the urgencies of the match, neither getting involved nor showing any emotional commitment. Even though he was technically qualified, his indifference meant he was low down on the technical staff's preference list. After a series of consultations, Albert believed his attitude was down to a high, self-imposed demand to do everything to perfection and be seen as one of the best in his position.

Acting in this manner, he provoked an obsessive mechanism of isolation of his affects, which blocked the emotional fuel needed to get angry, fight and give his all, taking risks. His determination not to fail ended up being counterproductive; he neither took a risk nor gained anything from a match. Metaphorically we can say that pressure "was eating him". Subjugation to his ideals was coming at a high price. After several sessions, I managed to break, in part, that mechanism of dissociation and isolation so that even if he had to endure mistakes he could add more fire and enthusiasm to his game. That change was well received by his teammates and coach, and enabled him to play with more continuity, be more confident, take risks, and assist goals, which he didn't dare to do before.

External component

By external component we mean those significant "others" in the life of players. They include the technical staff, the family (parents or spouse) and in another dimension the fans and the press.

It's a difficult art for a trainer to ensure that his players feel motivated and protected and receive an appropriate amount of pressure. In fact, this is a very important area for psychological work, since many trainers feel overstretched by their own demands, which they sometimes transfer to the players under the form of coercion or contradictory demands. They can do this with gestures, attitudes and often silences that are not understood. In a psychological sense they abandon their players, who end up fearing or hating them. Even though there might be players who are motivated by this, for the majority it's much more desirable that the trainer can communicate his demands in a harmonic and gradual way. Maturity is required in this area, which is the result of age but also of sporting experiences that trainers go through.

Parents and family are of major importance in a healthy sport career where a player also aspires to be successful. The looks and comments before and after a game and the expectations and hopes that are so many times unconsciously incorporated usually generate a constant degree of pressure, and family are able to provide emotional support. Parents and relatives often share in the glory and efforts of an athlete and are often the economic recipients of the achievement of ideals, with many athletes dedicating their careers to improving the quality of life for their loved ones. Even if feeling indebted carries a certain weight, generating pressure, it can also serve as stimulus and incentive. We can illustrate this with an interview with Michael Phelps regarding his future, after he had won his eighth Olympic medal in Beijing:

> Now I'll go on a holiday with friends, but my mom already asked me to start training for the 2009 World Cup because she wants to go to Italy. "I'm also pressured by her", said Michael Phelps, who next year will compete in the swimming contest in Rome by request of his mother. (*La Nación*, 2008b)

When a member of the family intervenes more actively, serving as a trainer, agent or critic, traps can appear that for many are difficult to solve, even if in a few cases a successful career may result. This can be perceived in the interview with Martina Hingis carried out by David Menayo in *Marca* on 26 September 2007:

Interviewer: How do you manage having your mother as your trainer?
Martina: My mother exerts a great influence on my game. She knows my tennis from outside and has helped me to reach the top. She's my mother outside the court and my trainer inside it and we manage to maintain a good relationship in both areas.

... She flees from the depressive image that chased some adolescent prodigies like the American Jennifer Capriati who, after family pressure and the circuit, ended up being accused of shop-lifting and using drugs, plunging into a profound crisis that still persists ("Shouldn't you lose weight to better your game?", a journalist asked her before she burst into tears).

Can one's own teammates become a source of pressure? Undoubtedly, when you have the feeling that others are watching out for your mistakes in order to grab your place on the team it can generate insecurity and great pressure when playing. The same effect can result when a player receives comments or judgements with respect to how he played; when he sees facial expressions of disapproval and receives personal rebukes for situations where the whole team was put at risk (mistakes, expulsions, substitutions, or the abandonment of different teammates during the course of the game).

If a player is included in a sub group—if he has friends he can talk to, share anecdotes with and argue with—he will feel less isolated in his problems, relieving the sensation of pressure. Similarly, having star players as teammates can be useful in order to play in a more carefree manner, as long as the player doesn't try to compete or be more than his star teammate. The media also plays its part in generating atmospheres, with their comments, articles, and interviews with athletes. Whether they are complimentary or critical, friendly or hateful in their comparisons they can become an added burden and their influence will vary according to the importance the players assign to these matters.

Let's consider an example provided by Grant Hughes for the *Bleacher Report*, April 2015:

In the ensuing months, the Warriors adopted a style of play that was joyously dominant. They destroyed opponents by huge margins, oftentimes toying with them for quarters at a time before blowing contests open with staggering stop-and-score runs. Whichever hacky clichés you liked—Golden State was using cheat codes, the Warriors looked like men among boys, etc.—they all applied. But now, with the playoffs right around the corner, the real pressure begins.

That pressure is tied directly to the Warriors' supreme regular season. Treat a league of motivated professionals like overmatched amateurs for six months, and a championship becomes the natural expectation. Obliterate the regular season, and you're supposed to crush the playoffs. Nothing less than the full weight of history is pressing down on the Warriors.

As a further example, we can consider the case of the football player Petr Cech, taken from the *London Evening Standard* (Johnson, 2013):

> Petr Cech admits Chelsea's players are struggling to deal with the pressure of salvaging their season by finishing in the top four and winning the Europa League. Cech said: "We are in a position where we fight for everything. We have a lot of pressure playing in the Europa League because we obviously want to win it. Every League game we are in the fight for the top four places and it's very tight there."
>
> Chelsea take on Basle in their Europa League semi-final first leg on Thursday and Cech (right) says it is hard for the squad, who have already played 61 games this term, to get a break from the strain. He said: "We are under pressure in every game, so you need to find the time to relax. We try to do so, step by step."

Fans, through their encouragement and support, make it possible for many players to loosen up and move more freely. On the other hand, there are players who will be affected negatively by this support, feeling more demanded upon, particularly when they are playing at home, with their own public, a situation that can worsen if their play awakens hostile chants or incidents. For many teams, the aggression of rival fans increases the group's cohesion and acts as a spur to confront adversity with courage and determination. The following case illustrates this point:

> Those who watched last night's match, between Cyprus and Portugal, witnessed a particular phenomenon that can be hard to understand. During the entire game, Cypriot fans booed Cristiano Ronaldo and shouted Lionel Messi chants to provoke CR7. He replied: "your love makes me strong, your hate makes me unstoppable". (Ronaldo7.net, 2011)

As far as the importance of events goes, a World Cup or the Olympic Games is supposedly the pinnacle of glory and to win in these competitions is the greatest aspiration of any athlete. The expectation level these events generate is enormous. It ceases being about only one player and his ability but rather a national team as a whole. It must be assumed that those who participate have been previously exposed to similar events by their clubs, federations, or youth teams. A good example is provided by the following article in relation to Asafa Powell, the Jamaican sprinter:

> Manuel Pascua, the Spanish trainer who turned Francis Obikwelu into the great African sprinter, believes that Powell's defeat in the 100 metre dash in Beijing was as predictable as his evolution: "I expected Asafa to reach 9,70s [he made 9,72s two weeks ago] and that he would fail at the games because he can't stand pressure. It often happens with athletes like him, they think too much". (Torres, 2008)

Groups with more experienced athletes or players, and with technical staff alert to emotional or psychological matters, make it possible to share and relieve the sensation of pressure to a great extent. Family support (parents, siblings, friends) is essential even if from a distance (telephone, internet), to modulate pressure by way of advice. It's important that a player enjoy and benefit from his aptitude and sport skills. The "deification" and idealisation that usually comes from outside via fans and the media can encourage a feeling of omnipotence ("I can have anything I want", "I have no limits"). Here a player must discriminate between the ideal as placed on him and falling for his own aggrandisement.

Pressure during the game

The reality of playing a game as part of a competition (for example, a World Cup match) stands in contrast with what is imagined about it in advance. The fact that a team may include many experienced players who will have played at this level before will serve as a pressure buffer for the younger and less experienced players. The trainer also plays this role.

When too much is expected of a player, he becomes "loaded" with pressures and demands, which can produce an inhibitory effect. For example, what happened to the All Blacks, for years the best rugby team in the world? How can we explain that after their win in the inaugural World Cup in 1987, their performance decreased at decisive moments and they were not crowned champions? Was it because being considered the favourite to win and feeling obliged to win became a pressure that inhibited them? Or, on the contrary, did they feel too relaxed and superior to other teams, meaning they consequently lacked the motivation to try their hardest? This all changed in 2011, when they hosted and won the championship and they repeated victory in 2015 in England.

Jorge Búsico, a sports journalist who specialises in rugby, comments that issues related to the game, to idiosyncrasy and pressure, must be addressed. Búsico adds that for New Zealanders rugby is the icon, the symbol that represents them throughout the world. To speak of New Zealand implies rugby and the All Blacks. Being favourites and "eating their rivals" can, for both the players and the technical staff, result in an increase in expectation that must be met. Pressures can prevent or inhibit players from choosing the best options. For the technical staff, this is reflected in the choice of tactics and strategies and who should be substituted during the game.

For the players, pressures are revealed when, for example, they don't take advantage of certain situations or choose the wrong moment to make a certain move. For example, during the World Cup held in France in 2007, the All Blacks, losing against France 20–18, made twenty-five phases during the last play, without using the drop, which if they had scored would have given them the victory; they finally used it badly after unsuccessfully trying to physically break their rivals in order to obtain a try. It must also be mentioned that the team didn't experience a negative reaction from the crowd regarding the drop; perhaps at home, playing for their regular clubs, they would be booed instead of cheered, but this concerned a World Cup. It should be noted that similar situations regarding tactical options and ways of choosing sport captains, added to matches being played on a rival pitch, arbitrary mistakes, etc., resulted in losing other World Cups. Things changed in 2011 and since then, they have won on home ground and away (England, 2015). What becomes evident is the need to realise how emotional and psychic factors influence sport results, even though the players might be in optimal physical shape and have top technical skills.

On the pitch, those who impose their tactics and dominate the game will pass on the pressure to their rivals. Pressure is an obligation/demand that must be complied with. The player who feels content with his performance will concentrate on other things like physical and strategic tactics. This gives an advantage over a player who still has to deal with his own phantoms.

Let's consider the case of a team that is winning but is intimidated by its rival and ends up tying or losing altogether. How can we understand what happened with Milan at the Champions League final against Liverpool, when they were winning 3-0 but were later tied before finally losing due to penalties? Does the explanation for such unexpected wins lie only in the fact that the favourites were slacking off, having already considered themselves the winners? In any case, turning disadvantage and the position of underdog into an incentive and mixing it with the "hunger for glory" can be a recipe for success.

During the Argentine football championship, a first division team (Gimnasia & Esgrima) played to maintain its category against a second division team (Atlético Rafaela), losing 3-0. How was it possible that Gimnasia should make a late comeback 3-0 during the second game against Atlético to avoid being relegated in the 2009 Apertura Tournament? Checking the news story regarding the Gimnasia match, I noted that there were only eighteen minutes left to score three goals in order to turn things around. In addition, the team were left with nine players with five minutes still to go. Mission impossible? This team and its trainer continued playing (they had faith, hope) even while exposing themselves to further goals from their opponents. A further incentive to fight for a win, aside from facing relegation, could have been that their traditional city rival was playing in the Libertadores Cup and was readying itself to have a double celebration: winning the cup and witnessing the fall of their biggest rivals.

Pride and anger must have transformed into competitive aggression, but this needed the complement of the opponents' downfall; the goalkeeper could not keep out goals from the forwards, plus a static defence and a panicked reaction after the first goal meant that Gimnasia were victorious.

As I mentioned in previous chapters, the validation method of theoretical hypotheses must be based on data from an experiential or a clinical reality. Going back and forth between theory and experience is what allows us to increase our knowledge. For this reason, I found it necessary to interview players who were in that football match. I transcribe below the talk held on 17 March 2010, with Fabricio Fontanini, at the time a defender for Atlético Rafaela:

R: What happened to you?

F: Something very strange. To be turned around in a few minutes. They talked of having bought our players, I don't know about that. What's more, I didn't think it possible that someone could reach a defining instance like the one we had and sell himself or betray his team. For me, there's no explanation.

R: How did it start?

F: When we received the first goal, when they made it, we told ourselves, they're coming down on us with all they've got! Immediately they made the second one, they seemed to be everywhere. That's it, we thought. Our bodies didn't respond, we seemed defeated, as if it was the same whether we lost or not. They kept on coming and were going to make the third goal any moment, without a doubt, we felt it as a premonition. Nobody could stop it. We didn't have an answer even though we wanted to give our all. We all kept ourselves at the back holding on until the next goal. During those moments, it seemed as if we were asleep.

R: Did it ever strike you that promotion was too much for you?

F: No, never. We spoke amongst ourselves and said that if we held on during the first half without receiving any goals, we'd be fine. And after that, after 35 minutes of the second half passed, we thought that we had it made.

R: And ...?

F: During those last few minutes we were paralysed.

R: Did you have that feeling in any previous game and, if so, did anyone try to help you break away from that state?

F: No. It didn't cross our minds that something like that could happen.

R: When the team found itself in difficult situations, who provided support?

F: We relied on ourselves.

R: Were there any leaders, inside or outside the stadium?

F: There were three or four who were the ones with the most experience, the older ones.

R: What happened with those leaders during this match?

F: They were all silent. We were as if paralysed.

R: So something like this had never happened before. It was totally unexpected.

F: We could have never imagined it.

R: It was the impact, then, the surprise effect?

F: Yes, it was a surprise. And after that we gave in. We felt the body harden, blocked. Something very strange.

R: When did you notice that sensation?

F: The paralysis? When they made the second goal. Instead of going out and making one ourselves, we didn't have any time to think when the second one came.

R: Nevertheless, you're used to playing or occasionally receiving a goal or two. That can come as no surprise, it can happen.

F: It's that we had such an advantage during the first part of the game. We thought it was ours … And that they could make three goals in seventeen minutes … it was totally unexpected.

R: From what you say, perhaps you prematurely rested on your laurels.

F: Perhaps. With the time that had passed, we thought the game was ours, that's why we fell asleep.

R: Mentally, you thought the game finished way before it actually was.

F: I hadn't thought of it that way but it's quite possible that we had begun to celebrate prematurely.

The value of this interview is that it provides elements to better understand what happened; at least as far as the second division team is concerned. A first observation is in reference to the "flight forward"; that is, considering the game is over way before the final whistle. Anticipating a win can be associated with the need to slacken the pace, due to very intense or perhaps excessive pressure. It implies a belief that the game is over, mission accomplished: I'll start to think about celebrating. It's a way of thinking that can make a player wish for a game to finish: I'm exhausted, I can't stand it any longer.

In this regard, the interview with the coach of Atlético Rafaela, Carlos Marcelo Fuentes, held on 20 March 2010, is significant. He made several observations as to what took place. First, he pointed out that the team was young, very committed, and generous. They didn't have many substitutes; so much so that during the match several young players made their debut on the bench. Even though they had overcome difficult tests in order to classify, during the away game they won 3-0, playing "the game of their lives". The level of commitment, perhaps excessive, tired them out physically and perhaps also psychologically. Perhaps for this reason there were three or four players that asked to be replaced almost simultaneously during the game's final leg, says Fuentes.

Many players were left with physical discomfort; they recovered and got ready to play three days afterwards, something that wasn't usual for them. They worked out a tactical plan—everything from balance to offensive positions. However, when I asked Fuentes if they had included how to react to possible disadvantage in case of conceding goals, he didn't mention any defensive schemes. We must also highlight his role as paternal leader of the team. During the second half of the last match, and after protesting to the referee to remove players from Gimnasia from the pitch, he was sent off and had to go to the changing room. The assistant coach was left in his place. At this stage, the score was 0-0 and he had only to wait for the end of the game to celebrate promotion to the first division.

I will concentrate my analysis on what appears as a "surprise effect". Its symptoms are similar to what occurs during a panic attack (Rubinstein, 1998). In this scenario, the subject becomes psychologically and physically "paralysed". His defences become totally blocked and he will feel at the mercy of "having surrendered" to a traumatic situation that he can't resolve by himself. The surprise factor, which in this case is the first goal scored by Gimnasia, had an impact on Atlético Rafaela, who had already offered all that they had up to that moment. But we must add concepts from group psychology that are related to the effect leaders have as "binders" and guides of the group's goals. Some of the more experienced players were also probably affected by the unexpected events, and the manager had been sent off, which left the group without a leader. Whether the team consciously perceived this to be important or not, the help they would have needed was not available. Biblical and military examples (Judith and Holofernes) illustrate that the elimination of commanders provokes panic, chaos, and desertion in the troop. The final result for Atlético Rafaela was due to a wide range of factors (apart from the pressure and the surprise effect), among which we must point out the no less important element of chance; after all, quoting Fuentes, "this is football".

Particular ways of reacting to pressure

There are different ways of confronting pressure and of condensing experience. The stronger athletes tolerate, manage and even enjoy difficult competitive situations. Others, counting on a particular skill or "magic wand", put into practice the necessary attributes at the most difficult moment to stand out from the group. Great champions can do this because it's at that moment that they feel it's important to set themselves free and let go. They are the ones that can perform feats, displaying their skills where others doubt. At a group level, they are the necessary leaders, the ones who feel that they can do anything and don't need anyone's help; they overcome any misadventure and do not even lose when they play marbles. They spread their enthusiasm to their teammates, taking on the pressure of the group themselves, and with their determination they are capable of turning around unfavourable moments. We may surmise that they are put by their teammates in the place of the ideal, by a mechanism of identification. From this moment onwards, the effect of contagion—a mixture of group suggestion and hypnosis—takes place.

Another typology is represented by those who put themselves in a masochistic position of passive suffering before any demanding test, or complain about the pressures of their surroundings. In these cases, experiences of tension, anguish or fear do not manifest at the mental or psychological level, but at the body or behavioural level. We observe states of recklessness, before or during the sporting event. This becomes evident in the following behaviours: 1) the subject is more aggressive with rivals, which leads to sanctions (warnings, expulsions) detrimental to themselves as well as their team; 2) they show intolerance towards their teammates, reprimanding them for mistakes, blaming them or shouting at them; 3) they argue with judges and referees until they are sanctioned; 4) they make mistakes, which can only be explained as a result of pressure. This leads to not being able to think either tactically or strategically. An example in the case of football could be the inability to decide whether to keep the ball or pass it, or make changes regarding the tempo of the game, and make moves that favour the action of the rival (bad passes, delayed reactions, missed goal opportunities, etc.); players are demonstrating that wearing a certain football shirt (important club, national team) or playing decisive games can prove too much for them at that particular moment.

All these behavioural manifestations clearly express an overstretched state where athletes are confronted with demands perceived as excessive, and are unable to manage these situations. This distressing state has an impact on the control of impulses, which leads to aggression and poor psychomotor synchronisation (clumsiness) and affects the use of more abstract functions like synthesis, evaluation, and selection of options. All these are attributes and functions that become diminished by the effect of pressure.

How and when to work with pressure

It is always convenient before a match to go over this equation, particularly with those who are the most inexperienced or who are going through problems derived from the inability to withstand pressure. First, it's important to check who or what is causing the pressure and work over the contents. For example, what attributes does the rival possess or what situation increases the demand on a player? Second, in groups or teams, the action and belief in the leaders to lessen pressure exerts a great influence. It's important to find out what they think and believe, since this will substantially influence the group they are in charge of. These beliefs can be unconscious but be effectively transmitted by different signals. The trainer of Las Leonas Hockey Team provides a good example. He admitted that he thought the team was capable of being the fourth greatest in the world, and this is as far as they actually got. However, once he convinced himself and the team that they could be the best in the world, they succeeded in winning the championship.

We have to help players learn to recognise and, if possible, verbally express what happens when they say they don't feel anything but actually present indirect manifestations, as was previously mentioned— like reckless states or intense neurovegetative symptoms (headaches, nausea, vomiting, diarrhoea, cramps, excessive sweating) without any explanation. A suggestive and cathartic effect can be achieved that is based on the transference established; this can help to lessen the idealisation of rivals or situations. Seeing and highlighting a rival team's best attributes, including not only technical skills but also emotional capabilities, together with identifying weaknesses and difficulties, we can try to predict what to expect and what resources are available to confront them. We can analyse how demanding situations were resolved in past games and apply this to the situation at hand. With athletes frequently affected by pressurised situations, we can work procedurally throughout diverse moments and experiences, without them feeling pressured to obtain quick results.

CHAPTER SEVEN

Ideals

Ideals constitute a very rich and extensive field of analysis, not only with respect to athletes but all humans. We will find in them the fire that drives us to achieve results, make and withstand sacrifices, and sustain ideas, values or hopes beyond the imaginable. They are a key element to understanding our motivations and our apparently inexplicable emotional ups and downs, delights, and disappointments. We can add that a subject's set of ideals together with their set of values, govern acts, feelings and conduct within his or her culture, and are responsible for the way in which a subject is regarded within a historical/cultural chain. The study of ideals reveals aspects that are intimately related to our early ways of seeking self-esteem. In order to understand this, we must go back to early childhood.

We find that the love lavished by parents on their children constitutes that which will endow an individual emotionally; that love, a mixture of the parents' awareness of the infant and egotistical love for them, is the last bastion of desire for immortality, of an extension of themselves in time. This is an unconditional love and, by the very fact of being and existing, doesn't require any counterpart on the part of the infant: the baby is wanted regardless of what he does to be desired. "His majesty", the baby, is gifted with all the virtues and perfections that the parents attribute and egotistically project on him, but how this love is perceived and experienced will change as the child grows older.

> In the next phase, the baby will realize that he is wanted and loved as long as he fulfills certain conditions. The parents will be perceived as objects to be desired or rejected and, together with the internalization of their attitudes, a function of auto-evaluation will start to be incorporated. What must be done to secure approval and what to obtain rejection. (Bleichmar, 1981, pp. 64–69)

In addition, the fact that the father also exists must also be taken into account; it will mark on the child's mind the presence of a third party. The father will be the rival that will compete with him for the preference of the loved object, the mother, marking a field where he will feel preferred or relegated. This will provoke, apart from rivalry, feelings of jealousy, of being an excluded third party, of fighting to the death in order to put himself in the preferred place as the only one, the winner. Finally, some children have access to another stage, where it is possible to accept that more than one person can occupy a place of preference. He is wanted as a son, for example, and someone else is desired for other emotional needs (as a husband, father or brother). A logic of conjunction prevails and not one of exclusion.

Let's consider, then, how a subject attempts to embody an ideal. This occurs at the moment when the subject stops being unconditionally admired and an object of perfection; he becomes someone who is being asked to adjust to certain norms. The ideal arises from a claim on the infant, moulded by his environment. The ideal is formed by a subject's disillusionment with the parents and the attempt to win once again the admiration of those he cares about by adjustment to the way in which he's judged. In other words, the attempt to embody an ideal is an attempt to recuperate the unconditional but lost love of early childhood.

The relationship the subject has with his ideals is similar to that which he has with the objects of love. Since the ideal generally appears in relation to concrete persons, it is assumed that it is possible for him to love those who embody his ideals as well; this is wisely reflected in popular aphorisms like "he fell in love" or "he betrayed his ideals".

Two other factors intervene in the embodiment of an ideal. First, the subject will try to win love in order to be accepted. Second, he will try to comply with social norms for fear of being punished. The latter regards meta-ideals, which are observance rules. A person's sense of satisfaction and self-esteem will depend on how he engages with meta-ideals, which are the rules that regulate his relationship with his ideals. These rules are, in fact, formed in childhood and establish how someone must behave in order to be valued or preferred; a kind of instruction or code about how to emotionally react when we contrast with the ideal.

If we define the ideal as a point on a scale, the meta-ideal will regulate how close a subject is to embodying it, resulting in feelings of acceptance, appreciation, and love the closer the subject is to the ideal, or rejection, hate, and denigration the further away the subject is from the ideal. Ideals in themselves can vary and be modified throughout one's lifetime, whereas the meta-ideals are usually much more stable and fixed (Bleichmar, 1981, pp. 66–69).

Now let us analyse what happens in the case of athletes. Some will receive even before they are born a desiring mark from the mother, father or extended family, with regards to becoming a player or athlete. Some parents who were athletes themselves might seek to constitute a form of continuity, expecting their offspring to replicate their success or succeed where they failed in order to satisfy their own unfulfilled wishes. What happens in this case is that the parents project their own ideals, identifying their son according to themselves. This will result in the child unconsciously carrying the burden of expectation, until, at best, he can confront it with his own wishes and hopes and make his own choices. Failure to do so will result in conflict and symptoms that we can try to resolve.

When a child is overestimated by his parents in their belief that he will fulfil their hopes, I am very far from believing that this is an expression of love towards him. There is a significant gap between that deceptive esteem, full of ideals, and realistic love. I highlight this point because it will become the source of countless failures, disappointments and disillusions of many aspirants who are not who their families think they are and who do not have the confidence to be the people they really are (unidealised).

We can observe a conflict area that frequently arises between parents and trainers. The latter complain that parents pressure them to make their sons or daughters the best; have a meteoric rise to sports stardom, devour rivals, break records, and reach the podium. These expectations, however, motivated by ambition and unrealistic goals, are almost impossible to fulfil. A budding athlete will have their aptitude and capacities continually put to the test by others. The frustration and sense of impotence this can provoke in many parents is usually badly tolerated, with reactions of anger and the denigration of trainers, doctors and even their own sons or daughters. It's worth pointing out how this occurs much more frequently with individual sports (tennis, golf) rather than with collective sports, where the peer group serves as the necessary contrast to distinguish the real and objective from where the subject finds him- or herself.

What is the usual path of an aspiring athlete? He or she will count on a kind of platform consisting of:

a) personality traits (disposition, genetic and congenital factors),
b) the family and rearing stage,
c) the sporting skills and abilities that became entrenched by training centres, joining institutional competitive groups or social relationships in the sport microworld.

Many athletes are born with an aptitude or skill for a certain discipline or they discover, learn and develop attributes along the way (at school, in clubs, or in the neighbourhood). This will gradually give them self-esteem as well as pleasure. They will be regarded and recognised by others who will admire their talents, and for this reason a sporting discipline will be loaded with special significance, placing the athlete in a privileged position. Much later on, when the moment of retirement arrives, the athlete must be able to endure the loss of such a place of privilege. Consequently, it will be desirable that the athlete sustain the base of his or her self-esteem in other areas to enrich him or her as a person.

The next step is the training, both physical and mental. This will imply dedication and the investment of time, effort, and also money. At the same time, it will include giving up time otherwise spent on family, study, and recreational activities with friends. Even though the first part of training will have come from what has been incorporated at home with one's family, sport centres, schools and clubs will add, through their technical staff, schemes and styles that will greatly influence what each athlete searches for in order to achieve his or her goals.

To illustrate this point we'll examine two styles of play. The first highlights the ludic or pleasurable aspect of sport, which includes winning or losing as part of what can naturally occur; where rivals can also be mates and colleagues in a game where everyone participates, and where goals scored are non-competitive and the game is played on the basis of psychological and sporting maturity. The experience, regardless of the results, serves to teach the players how to improve. The experiential atmosphere that is generated will influence the mood of the player and also the results. For the other style of play a philosophy predominates where winning is the only thing that matters, and not doing so, or not being number one, is synonymous with failure. The sport career is a war against everyone, where not only the most capable survives, but also the most cunning and deceitful. There is no room for friendship, only strategic or incidental allies. The more time it takes to reach the goal, the more wasted it's considered. Interest and material ambition prevail over honour and glory. It's a more selfish model, where others are a means to achieve the desired end. There are no debts of gratitude.

Taking into account what has been previously mentioned—competing in tournaments, tough training, and technical, physical, tactical and mental maturity—occasional trips and changing teams, mates and technical staff will become common occurrences. Some athletes will reach positions of relevance; they will be the ones who get to the top, the ones who succeed. In these cases we can make reference to the tripod model (following Kohut's ideas) that guides and sustains the will and ego of the player or athlete, regardless of failures and misfortunes.

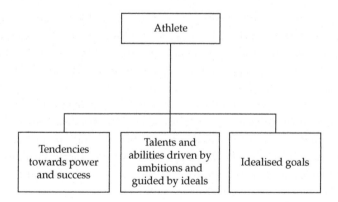

We can observe a particular tendency towards power and success, which will combine with the impulse offered by personal ambitions. This psychological fuel will be supported by the talents and abilities that have been perfected, developed and exploited throughout the entire formative period. There is still another necessary ingredient, which is the firm belief that the goals set will be reached. This will help an athlete to withstand all the sacrifices and frustrations endured. Some will be able to cope on their own; others will rely on the invaluable presence of loved ones or trainers that believe in them.

Lastly, I must include an aspect common to many athletes, which is the heroism of their achievements. This is highlighted by the media and alludes not only to the effort employed in obtaining one's objective but also to the drama involved in overcoming difficulties in order to achieve it. The athlete will sum up the values recognised by the social setting to which he belongs and this will embody his ideals. In this way, heroism is the result of the athlete's actions as well as the value others bestow on him. At the level of myth, the hero will be the one who replaces the pre-existing ideal by means of parricide, arrogating to himself the feat that was an achievement of the group; he is the one who embodies, as mentioned, the ideals and values appreciated by the group. These, and no other, are the "garments" worn by many successful athletes.

The following articles illustrate athletes expressing their satisfaction of having achieved their goals (obtaining an Olympic medal, for example) and the social consequences (at the national and local level) of having fulfilled the ideal.

From *The Guardian* online 19 August 2008:

> In a manner every bit as emphatic as Usain Bolt's 100 metres victory on Saturday Yelena Isinbayeva last night proved herself the greatest female athlete of her generation. Isinbayeva won a second consecutive gold in the pole vault and broke her world and Olympic records in the process.
>
> The final had been billed as a showdown between Isinbayeva, the Russian, and the United States' Jennifer Stuczynski. There was certainly a fierce rivalry between them but not much of a contest. After winning the US Olympic trials this year Stuczynski threw down a challenge to Isinbayeva: "I hope we go over there and do some damage, kick some Russian butt", she said.
>
> The two women had played cat-and-mouse with each other throughout the final but there was no question who the cat was. For the first 90 minutes of the competition Isinbayeva did not attempt a vault but sat trackside, her baseball cap pulled down low over her eyes. When the bar reached 4.70 m she decided to stop passing and

cleared the height at her first attempt. By that point seven of the 12 competitors had been knocked out.

After tugging her cap back on to her head she sat down again and passed on the next two heights, watching as Stuczynski moved into first place at 4.80 m. When Isinbayeva rose for her second vault of the evening she and the American were the only athletes left in the competition.

Soon she had the stage to herself. Stuczynski failed at 4.90 m and Isinbayeva had only herself to compete against. She had already attracted the loudest welcome of any foreign athlete at the meet, louder even than Bolt in the 200 m second round.

"I was trying to do my best for the crowd," she said afterwards. "It makes me happy, so happy, I felt that I could not go out without the world record because of the support the crowd gave me." (Bull, 2008)

A further example, regarding Novak Djokovic, from the *Daily Mail* (2011):

Around 100,000 tennis fans gave Novak Djokovic a royal reception in his nation's capital Belgrade after the 24-year-old arrived home in Serbia to celebrate winning his first Wimbledon title.

Djokovic, who leapt to the top of the ATP rankings in the process, was greeted by a deafening roar as he arrived in an open-top bus which took hours to reach the Serbian parliament square from the airport.

Traffic on the main motorway ground to a halt as fans got out of their cars to salute Serbia's most popular athlete, whose entire family paraded alongside him on a giant stage where rock bands entertained the crowd.

The following excerpts from *The Guardian* online concern a Buckingham Palace reception for Britain's Olympic and Paralympic medallists:

Boxer Nicola Adams, whose nifty footwork helped power her to a historic gold, had been in training for the reception hosted by the Queen: "It was excellent. I was excited and nervous all at the same time. But I got my curtsey right so that was OK. I'd been practising".

On life after the Games, Adams said: "I've been here, there and everywhere. In a helicopter, in Rio with the prime minister and now I'm topping it all by meeting the Queen."...

British Paralympic Association chief executive Tim Hollingsworth said: "Our medalists are honoured to attend today's royal reception and it constitutes another memorable occasion for those who helped to make 2012 a year in which Great Britain has been so hugely proud of the achievements of our Paralympic and Olympic athletes." (Davies, 2012)

And from the *ABC Grandstand* website, regarding the honour of Australian Olympians:

Sydney has come to a standstill for the first official welcome-home parade for Australia's Olympic team after the London Games. Thousands of fans lined George Street to watch the procession, which began just after noon (AEST).

More than 100 athletes received a rousing reception as they made their way from Circular Quay to Town Hall. Twelve Olympic gold medalists took part, including cyclist Anna Meares and swimmer Alicia Coutts.

The team was given the keys to the City of Sydney during an official ceremony at Town Hall after the parade. Basketball bronze medalist and Australia's flag-bearer in the opening ceremony, Lauren Jackson, accepted the keys from Lord Mayor Clover Moore on behalf of the team ...

Ms Moore said the parade and presentation of the keys of city was a fitting tribute to the team. "It is ceremonial and it is symbolic and it is a way of saying you are very, very special and you'll receive the keys to the city and it is a great honour," she said. (Browning, 2012)

Michael Phelps talked to *La Nación* after winning multiple gold medals at the Olympics:

The wonder boy from Baltimore arrived here with a very clear objective and he fulfilled it: "I wanted, literally, to do something with this sport which no one had done before. My wish was to be an Olympic champion, to be remembered together with names like Mark Spitz,

Jesse Owens, Carl Lewis. That was my dream ... and I don't know what to say, I can't find the words", he said yesterday.

"Congratulations, but now you'll have a great responsibility. you'll be an example for millions of people", his countryman Spitz told him, even though the comparison between the two becomes difficult, since Phelps has to live his feat during a much more media-centered and competitive period.

"I want to be the first Michael Phelps and not the second Mark Spitz. I will never stop saying that what Spitz did for swimming was amazing and I still believe it", expressed today's hero, who even received a phone call from George W. Bush: "If you managed to win eight gold medals, you can win anything", said the president of the United States.

One thinks that this shouldn't be the moment to worry about what will happen. Nevertheless, Bob Bowman, trainer of Phelps, knows very well that this can't stay this way. He has already started to find ways of motivating him, to go for more glory. "During the next four years I would like to try some new tests—said the multiple medalist. Trials which I haven't run yet and afterwards we'll see what happens. Bob told me that he wanted to try new training methods, things that we haven't done before. They will be four fun years", he predicted. (Trenado, 2008)

Can ideals end up having a traumatic effect on an athlete?

The dissemination of sport and its practice on a mass scale has taken place only in the last few decades. The increasing number of amateur and professional players has brought new and varied issues to light. The athlete's family group has also presented new conflicting situations, which have to be categorised and confronted effectively. We can observe with regards to high competition how aspirations and ideals become a source of conflict. The effect of this is frequently alienating and impacts on the mind and body of players.

To illustrate, we will study a paradigmatic and hypothetical case: Alfred, twenty-eight years old, sought a consultation because a friend of his whom he hadn't seen for a long time found him to be very depressed. Although not convinced, he nevertheless made an appointment with me and arrived to the first session a bit crestfallen; his appearance was ungainly despite his athletic demeanour, and his sorrowful state was hard to conceal. He expressed his uneasiness and the anxiety that had taken hold of him. He confessed to being plagued by his predicament: even though he was still young, as an athlete he was already considered to be old, only a few steps from retirement. He was hungry for victories, but his career had been marked by one frustration after another, with only scarce moments of sunshine in his life. He was in a hurry to get out of his present state, but at the same time greatly distrusted the usefulness of psychological intervention. He supposed this came from his family, since his mother had become resentful over the therapeutic outcome for one of his sisters, who did years of therapy but nevertheless ended up in a psychiatric institution.

I was struck by his inner anguish and the type of conflict that he faced. Admittedly, this is a typical consequence of the limited time frame an athlete has to enjoy a sporting career. I asked myself how long he would give me to try to help him to … it remained in that moment an open question, help him to do what?

He told me about his beginnings with tennis, accompanying his older brothers and father to the club until he started playing with them and began to acquire a taste for it. When they realised he showed an aptitude for tennis he started to practise more regularly, taking classes, receiving training, and eventually competing and winning children's tournaments. When he was about fifteen, they decided that he should travel to a neighbouring country in order to attend a training centre. As he began to improve, so did the attention of his family, on the lookout for triumphs. At social gatherings, everything revolved around his skills, his possible meteoric rise, and the hopes that everyone placed on seeing his name making newspaper headlines. His family were eager for him to compete in other countries. With difficulty, he managed to come to terms with the first migration, but later had to travel once again. This time it involved adapting to a new language, hotel and city, and rivals who only wanted to defeat him. Alfred wanted to travel with someone he trusted, someone who could contain and guide him. After all, he was only a teenager. Nevertheless, the money wasn't there to pay for someone who could provide this. He ended up travelling by himself and talking to his family a lot on the phone. Undoubtedly the expectations placed on him were already taking their toll, especially because he was carrying that load by himself.

Alfred began to lose rapidly in tournaments. He also confessed that "the loneliness was unbearable"; "so much so that I told the trainer that I couldn't stand it any longer and I came back". At that stage, his coach decided not to continue with him. "I must have disappointed him, but he also let me down, he abandoned me, but I must admit he was good in other ways, he made me advance a lot in the ranking".

Was it the trainer who had abandoned him? What about his parents and siblings? Alfred didn't dare require more of their presence and companionship. He had a model, which his father often made reference to, of how good it had been for him to get away from the family when he had to attend high school in a nearby town. That made him stronger, enabling him to overcome difficulties; in short, become a man. That was the path he had had to follow, the identification and the ideal, but became distrustful and emotionally introverted, character traits that Alfred suffered as affective deficiency during childhood.

Meanwhile, the family, in particular his father and elder brother, tormented him:

> It was a constant pressure. When we spoke on the phone after a game, they reproached me that I had everything to win but didn't do so, that all their expectations were placed on me, that they had invested thousands of dollars and all to no avail. If I realised I was no good, it would be better, according to them, to do something else. I felt that their lack of confidence was deadly. I went out to play but inside I was full of anger and impotence. It also made me feel useless and lonelier than ever. When I mentioned this to my next trainer he told me that all this was the result of my immaturity; I shouldn't phone my home any more or worry about what they said.

The economic situation also generated pressures. Since Alfred never won, he couldn't obtain enough money. His trainer wanted to get paid but his family would cut off his income. There were no sponsors so he had to look for cheaper trainers who were below his standards and compete in circuits that were more accessible but did not give him a high enough score to rise in the rankings. This only led to further anger, frustration, and impotence. Nevertheless, Alfred tried his luck in tournaments in the northern hemisphere but the vicious cycle only repeated itself with changes in trainers, tournament categories, etc., reprimands and demands for results from family, and his loneliness and the feeling that he just couldn't succeed—all being his fault.

It was inevitable at this stage that his predicament would be further complicated by physical injuries. The shoulder, the knees, ankles and elbows took the brunt of his misfortune, with the added complication of several operations, rehabilitation, and months without playing or generating earnings. His parents, far from helping him, continued to hammer him with their belittling discourse, which only increased his already low self-esteem.

It is worth highlighting the psychosomatic functioning throughout this situation. It seems almost inevitable that the frustration that couldn't channel itself satisfactorily in external reality, unable as well to be psychologically metabolised, used the body as an outlet. The shoulders, ankles, and knees, which serve as support and the most likely places to get hit, were precisely the places where the injuries appeared.

We can understand that the injuries were the product of all the conflicting drama that Alfred suffered. He felt beaten, and overcome with rage, impotence, and pain. In a general state of decline and with little energy, he got tired easily, sad, and unable to think. He was almost led to believe that he had an unknown illness; he wanted to identify the bug that was making him sick and had several check-ups, but nothing was found.

To this scenario I must add that outside of sport his life was quite bleak. He continued to be very dependent emotionally and economically on his parents; he had few friends and had had hardly any long-term attachments. His sex life was poor and brief—far from the fantasy of hundreds of beautiful girls, preferably models, hassling him and trying to conquer a tennis player of his age and with his looks. In addition, Alfred hadn't developed culturally or intellectually. Nor did he have any future projects; despite his age, he had been living and acting like a fifteen year old.

After several sessions, I asked myself once more how I could help him. I realised that my proposal had to be very clear and, if possible, brief and effective. I also knew that his problems wouldn't be resolved in a few sessions, but we had one thing in our favour; despite all his discomforts, Alfred yearned to improve his quality of life. If possible he wanted to improve his game, but he also wanted to grow as a person. He was conscious of how limited his existence had been. Nevertheless, he was a fighter who, despite his wounds, was prepared to face another battle, in this case an internal one, with his own phantoms. It was essential for him to understand that this time he wouldn't be left alone.

I found myself dealing with a person with depression (he was sad, apathetic, downcast). His problems were centred on himself and his self-esteem, with a very high ideal to fulfil, which was to become a tennis champion, a tremendous demand, and when it came to making assessments it was "all or nothing" for him. Alfred sensed that he had made the wrong choice; that his career had arrived at a point where there was no turning back and he would have to return home with his head hung low. His parents, in turn, would receive him, but he would have to pay a high price for not having satisfied everyone's expectations; he would be considered a failure. I observed that Alfred didn't know how to disentangle himself from this situation; he didn't have any personal resources, projects or alternatives on the horizon. It was important for me to know if there were any symptoms that remained from his injuries, if he would be limited in his game; I asked him to have a good clinical and orthopaedic check-up for which he got the all clear.

Once I decided what course to take therapeutically, I proposed organising a support team, which, like a safety net, could sustain him at critical moments. Since Alfred had a trainer, a nutritionist, a therapist, a doctor, an orthopaedist and his parents to determine what was best for him, I suggested that he coordinate and bring together these resources at his disposal. Focusing on the dialogue with those who took care of him, I managed to neutralise a sense of dispersion, which had operated in his psyche as a destabilising factor—lack of concentration etc. This greatly reduced Alfred's anxiety and consequently his mental dispersion. He noticed this immediately on the court, so much so that he got excited with the idea of returning to the professional circuit and making his last stand.

Alfred looked for my approval regarding his project, since he didn't have the consent of his parents. It was as if they simply pressed the "delete" button regarding anything he required or intended to do that didn't coincide with their plans for him. At this moment in time they were telling him not to invest one more cent in doctors, trainers, or trips. They proposed that he abandon everything and return home to help with the family business. Heaven forbid that he should be able to live his own life and come out of his predicament with the help of an outsider. Money was the excuse in their engulfing and endogamous intents.

Nevertheless, we decided that he had sufficient stamina and was still young enough to play tennis once again. This situation of well-being in the transference bond with the therapist, what is known as idealised transference, was apparent at this stage in the therapy. Alfred would comment: "I never felt so well understood. It's as if you were there with me, on the court" or "If I came here every day I would be unstoppable; the trouble is I'm not Federer, I don't have the means to pay you". We know that the other side of idealisation is persecution. For Alfred it was difficult to establish relationships with others and with himself in a realistic manner. Consequently, he wasn't objective about his friendships; people went from being God to Satan at the least setback, which meant he didn't have any friends (something quite difficult, anyway, in that competitive and individualistic world), despite years of being in the tennis circuit. Many were false and belittled him; they were certainly not worth befriending. As a result, Alfred lost out on certain feelings of fellowship, which would have helped to relieve his feelings of loneliness and abandonment when he was on tour. The signallings and interpretations in relation to these aspects were a significant part of the work that we tackled for about two months.

We also dealt with the ambiguous bond with his parents, whose influence weighed so much on him. We saw how, in fact, he unconsciously searched for them to tell him things that he knew would be hurtful. Despite the fact that he tried to make me give him a second option with regards to what he should do, I tried to develop in him a certain degree of autonomy and self-reflection. I wanted him to determine courses of action for himself as well as begin to deal with consequences and learn from his own mistakes instead of blaming others.

At a second stage, when he began to feel sure of himself and more confident, he recommenced his travels and tours. He won some games and found a good trainer, who bettered his game. As part of the therapeutic strategy, I went to see him in some tournaments and spoke to his trainer. The therapy sessions started to focus more on issues related to tennis; what happened on the court and technical and tactical issues, which Alfred expounded on and reasoned on during the session. Putting together what I had seen on the court and what he had told me during therapy, I noticed that it was very difficult for Alfred to win games and sets. He also had great difficulty "reading" the games, observing his opponent, and making use of this information in order to find a strategy for the match. He kept centring everything that occurred on himself, in an almost compulsive need for self-assertion and victory. Unable to find victory, he easily became frustrated, stumbling at times (mental blanks), which made him lose points.

At an objective level we observed the following facts and their unconscious dynamics: anger as a result of frustration, ambiguity with regards to his parents, an unbearable demand placed upon him to obtain victory, the desire to lose in order to be different from his parents, and the absence of an alternative between playing for himself and playing for his parents' ideal. This internal struggle made him lose concentration in the fight to gain points against his opponents: following the path of demand or voluntary concentration was not the way in which these conflicts could be resolved. His tendency to look inwards, obsessively over-elaborating everything, I countered with an exercise designed to "open his eyes"; I made him tell me without thinking everything that had happened (free association). Thus he began to really think about situations that he had previously overlooked, even though he had consciously registered them. For example, when telling me about a game with an opponent who hit one groundstroke after another, it became possible for him to think that if he loosened his return, made certain shots or varied the rhythm (a short one, a long one), he could complicate the rival's game. Up to this point, Alfred had always reacted like a mirror; if the rival hit groundstrokes he responded with even harder ones.

The above example clearly shows how easy it is to alienate and ensnare oneself, lose one's way for the sake of being lured by the call of modern sirens. We ask ourselves in what way, through what psychological mechanisms and from what stimuli and influences one arrives at this result.

We know that ideals are the product of family structures that, in turn, are impacted by a culture that promotes and promises huge gratifications like fame, success, or great sums of money to those who manage to reach the top. Similarly, for those from a low social class and with lower incomes, the high competition athlete is regarded as someone who is valued and will bring the possibility of social advancement and economic well-being to the whole family group. It is not a small matter to transform oneself into the hero, the saviour, the one who fulfils people's dreams, raising high the name of a town or a country; the one who changes the lives of his or her loved ones, making up for their former hardships. To achieve this, an athlete is prepared to sacrifice or relegate more basic needs like their social integration, studies, and close relationships, as well as a more integral development of their personality.

This set of circumstances affects the mind of a young athlete and their families. Everyone bets that those youngsters will follow a demanding and absorbing career, despite the fact that very few will reach their goal. The great majority of athletes, in fact, will find obstacles and trials along the way that they won't be able to overcome, and will fall by the wayside together with their aspirations. Entry into the circuit of high competition will make the tension between what is expected and what is actually possible turn into something dramatic. For many it will culminate in mental health problems, since it will be impossible to withstand the tension exercised on the body, mind and life of the player. This impact is defined as traumatic, injurious.

The search for stimuli or a substance (psychotropic or other types of drugs) that will help to relieve the pain of an injury are part of the answer at the physical level. However, symptoms of a more definite psychological disorder, like depression, lack of interest or motivation can also become evident as inhibitions during the game (lack of concentration, mistakes, lack of competitive aggression). If someone ends up giving up an activity for which he's highly skilled, for which he has an aptitude, and which he has been able to enjoy many times, feeling sadness and happiness, relief and regret simultaneously when withdrawing from the competition is normal. Behind all this, we can elucidate the presence of conflicts that reveal cannibalistic and unmanageable pressures intertwined with accepting or breaking with family mandates, demands that only lead to feelings of loneliness and lack of love when expected life goals are not met.

The behaviour patterns mentioned above, like many others, necessarily require the intervention of specialists that not only know how to work with cognitive aspects (concentration, attention) but also with the deeper unconscious that generates all the symptoms previously described. I observed a marked denial and resistance in sport circles to assimilate and include the resources that can help athletes, trainers and family members to improve the quality of life for our "modern gladiators".

To the methods of therapeutic intervention made explicit in the case of Alfred, we should also add being able to examine and work with ideals as part of the routine with any player or team by following some of these guidelines:

1. Discern the subject's expectations/ambitions from those of his or her loved ones (parents or those closest to the subject).
2. Find out from the trainer the athlete's skills and possibilities.
3. Analyse the successes and failures in other areas of the athlete's life to see how he or she reacted on those occasions. Check if there has been any variation throughout the subject's career or if he or she has always maintained the same standard of conduct.
4. Examine how much influence suggestion or criticism has on the athlete.

All these steps will allow us to know ideals and ways of relating to the athlete. It will be important to stress that which is procedural, remembering that self-esteem and courage don't play a part in just one test or match but are needed throughout a career. Therapy will lead to acting with objectivity, in a flexible and benevolent manner, without excluding constructive criticism.

CHAPTER EIGHT

Injuries

Injuries are part of what normally happens in the course of an athlete's career. They have their origin in traumatological mechanisms and there are also psychological reasons that account for them. Both of these factors interact, since we are a psychosomatic unit, in such a way that a permanent interaction exists between what happens in our psychic life and what consequently takes place in our body, just as what happens in our body will impact on our psyche.

There normally exists a harmony, an integration between the psychic and the somatic, which can be affected in the extreme in those cases that we refer to as psychosomatic illnesses. They are usually related to persons who have difficulty in verbally expressing their emotions. This characteristic, together with a certain constitutional tendency, leads to the channelling of emotional conflicts within the body.

The muscular-skeletal system is an athlete's working tool. It will therefore be the area with the highest degree of exposure or weariness. In addition, when there are tensions, pain and emotional conflicts, this system will be a privileged area for these characteristics to settle and express themselves.

With respect to the mechanical and traumatological causes that provoke injuries, this is mostly due to the muscular-skeletal and joint weariness provoked by the continuous use of areas of the body employed by the sport in question. The same occurs as a result of blows received from adversaries in those sports that involve collisions or direct friction with the opponent (rugby, football, basketball) or sports that use objects like sticks, mallets, and bats (hockey, polo, baseball). Other systems, like internal organs, are affected to a lesser degree.

Also, the continued use of certain body areas can reveal congenital deficits, which become apparent when a load or greater demand takes place, which otherwise would have remained asymptomatic. In each sport there are joints and muscular groups that are more frequently affected (tennis elbow, shoulders in volleyball, or inferior limbs in football). On the other hand, there are injures that occur due to the so-called "bad movements" or bad technique. These are the improper forcing of muscles, joints and tendons that oppose the physiology of the movement.

The injury will provoke a sudden break of the organic balance; as a result, sport practice will be limited and a period of time will be needed for recovery. Such a way of putting it, close to a "medical" conception, must be linked with the psychic notion of trauma, which, since Freud, moves away from the medical model. The psychological repercussions of an injury, which we call trauma, deserve consideration. First of all, a "punctual" trauma doesn't exist, which would be equivalent to saying he injures his knee, afterwards there is pain and psychological suffering added to the specific physical discomfort in the knee; instead, a traumatic situation is brought about. There are various concepts of a "traumatic situation" (Baranger, Baranger & Mom, 1988, pp. 113–128), which can make an explanation more complex; however, it is very useful to have one when it comes to choosing the most adequate approach to each particular case.

One line of thought is that the blow, fracture or injury occurs in a particular place by pure coincidence or a constitutional, genetic disposition exists making that part of the body more sensitive or debilitated. We must ask ourselves whether there were any previous injuries there and if so, how were they cured and what, if any, after-effects were experienced. Also, how did the athlete's parents react with respect to the injury? Did they help or were they paralysed? Did they blame their son? Did they punish him? Did they treat him like a king or like a total invalid? And the doctors, did they calm him down or provoke further stress? Did they prove trustworthy? All the related associations, memories and feelings will open like a fan in the mind of the player, influencing how and how much he will react with respect to what took place. He will also establish comparisons between those experiences and his current state.

Another line of thought will include how important the affected area is for the player and his performance. He will compare similar or equivalent injuries that his teammates had, with the resulting questions: how did they cope? To what extent did they recuperate? How did they cope with the waiting before they rejoined the team? Who treated them? On the other hand, it will be important to determine the amount of distress the injury provoked: did the subject feel very helpless? Did they consider that it wasn't very serious? Did they receive support? Were they teased about what happened to them? Were there any deadlines imposed? Undoubtedly, all this emotional background will be processed according to whether the player is going through a moment of more security, strength, and self-confidence. The injury and the traumatic process at the mental level will demand per se psychological work and internal proof of sufficiency.

We can also include here the fact of having to cope with dependencies and needs in order to turn to others that can help and protect an athlete. Finding oneself momentarily disabled and dependent on others, who make decisions and suggestions, is a difficult test for many athletes, who experience that state of need as an unbearable weakness (disablement trauma). To defend themselves, they will ignore prescriptions, try to manage independently, disagree with professional advice, or generate quarrels. Ultimately this can lead to resentment and have a bad effect on the injury, which might not heal properly (in appearance only, not at a psychic level).

Another view leads me to consider that, as a consequence of the injury, the athlete will experience a state of retraction and self-absorption. All interest will turn to the body and the affected area, turning the injury into an almost hypochondriac area of interest. Thoughts, ideas and affective reactions will all revolve around the damage suffered. Even though this reaction is almost universal, for athletes the load thrust upon their body is more intense, since this is their working tool and source of self-worth and self-esteem.

In light of the above, they will pay special attention to recovery times, the possibility of remaining disabled or fully recovering, the impact it will have on their body image, the effect the injury will have on their skills, as well as the costs (economic, sporting). We must therefore be alert in order to diagnose and work preventively with those who are most likely to suffer depression or a severe collapse of their self-esteem.

The relationship between the magnitude of the injury and the psychological traumatic response is revealed in cases with a bad injury but with little traumatic repercussion and vice-versa—athletes with minor injuries but with a tremendous psychological traumatic impact. The key to understanding this resides in the psychic repercussion, that interior and phantasmagoric factor triggered from the moment of injury or just after. The athlete's history of sport injuries on the one hand, and/or the psychological traumas on the other (losses, crises, breakups), as well as the way in which he has recovered from these occurrences, at the somatic as well as the psychic level, will have an impact on his way of responding, considerably increasing or reinforcing his fears or, on the contrary, muffling or cushioning them if circumstances are resolved more or less satisfactorily.

The fact that a surgical solution is required will add to the fear and anxiety that is produced. The athlete will confront his or her doubts and fears with regard to how much the operation will contribute or take away; the athlete will be trusting or suspicious in wanting to postpone the surgery or throw him- or herself into it, sometimes in a manic fashion. Let's consider an example: Edward, who is nineteen years old, is a first division football player who has an injury in his right knee that is becoming chronic. This complaint provokes discomfort when he plays; sharp sensations prevent him from giving himself completely to the game. Unfortunately, he receives contradictory advice from doctors who work for his club. One doctor tells him he should be operated on right away; another tells him that he should continue with the medical treatment without resorting to surgery. These conflicting opinions greatly increase his own doubts as to what course he should take. As a result, he starts to lose his place on the team along with the possibility of showing himself and his talents, and gradually he becomes absorbed in a state of depression and impotence, circumstances that lead to the suggestion that he should seek psychological help.

Edward, needless to say, is afraid of an operation and its after-effects, since he's not certain he will be completely rehabilitated. On the other hand, he can't go on in his current state. His fears increase because he suffers from an injury that is not common. He knows a teammate with more experience who has had a similar injury, but he shies away from him for fear of being seen as fainthearted, weak, unskilled, or annoying. His knee "hypochondria", self-absorption and brooding gradually sink him into a dead-end situation.

After a couple of interviews, I propose that he start talking not only to the more experienced teammate but also to players from other divisions who have suffered similar injuries. Edward is as hard as nails. It's very hard for him to accept something different, since he's distrustful and is very afraid at the same time. His self-image of strength doesn't admit too many fissures; he doesn't want to be seen in this predicament for much longer. My suggestion is an attempt to establish some kind of bridge that will break his isolation, making him feel acceptable after comparing himself with peers who have also been "temporarily injured". Moreover he could also incorporate their thoughts to evaluate how much and by what means they managed to recuperate themselves physically and mentally, as well as in terms of their football. At the same time, this strategy would distance him from his repetitive brooding, which is dragging him down time and again into states of complaint and despair.

Meanwhile, we start to explore the image he has of his body as a whole, how difficult it is for him to integrate the idea of temporary harm or injury with the importance and value he places on his knees in particular. In this case, the injury is not only stopping him from playing but also destroying his self-esteem, which is having an impact on his family group and wider social circle (brothers, friends, girlfriend). Edward feels that he is a disappointment and a failure to all those who have been sustaining and accompanying him throughout his sport life. To work out this issue through signalling and interpretations, together with his idealised representation of physical potency, is a necessary step in order to make his knee less of a burden, thus aiding the recuperation process. This is finally accomplished by complementing the psychological with traumatological and kinesic aspects.

Can a person injure him- or herself repeatedly because of psychological problems and not due to coincidence or accident? It would be like affirming that the cause of an injury is emotional. It's important to demolish the idea that it's either psychological or physical, taking one side or the other. Undoubtedly both intervene, since our way of functioning integrates the psychic with the somatic. Nevertheless, emotional states, worries, distress, fears, conflicts, when they reach a certain magnitude manage to impact on the muscular-skeletal system by way of the central nervous system. Movements, which take place when playing a sport, require preparation and top muscular tension. The latter will be influenced by circumstances characteristic of the competition and the life experiences of each player. Fear, anxiety and frustration, whether conscious or unconscious, as well as the significance that a certain rival or team acquire, can vary the muscular tone, producing hiccups (diminution) or asynchronic hypertonias (increase of muscular tone), depending on what the player needs to do at that moment. As a result, the kick, the blow, the pass, steps, turns or other movements that he or she does will result in areas of greater fragility or tendency to injury. This is even more evident in sports where friction with the opponent takes place. Excessively hardened or weak muscles in situations where there are clashes are conducive to injuries.

It's not true that emotional states can be completely blocked, enabling the athlete not to feel anything so that he or she can concentrate on the game. Perhaps some athletes have a greater capacity to dissociate themselves (operative dissociation), but with the risk of letting the body deal with it through functional disorders (cramps) or more serious injuries. What happens in high competition, when the defining stages of a tournament approach? The level of internal and external demand increases. Technical aspects even out, and each time, and more noticeably, the difference that the psychological aspect makes becomes decisive. All players throughout their career undergo thorough athletic training: hours of physical work, with gym and diet under the supervision of sport and physical trainers, physiotherapists, and nutritionists. We know that this only contributes to 50% of an athlete's performance. The other 50% corresponds to the mental or psychological aspect.

Disclosure, as well as being able to understand and use resources and professional support in this area, is very recent. What must be highlighted? Attention, memory, concentration, attitude, fighting spirit? It is convenient to include each one of these psychic functions, not isolated in themselves but articulated in the set of motivations, desires and pressures that appear within a specific context or situation. Particularly, motivation and its ups and downs within a game reflect a great many life experiences amongst which the following are included: confidence in one's own skills, calculating the rival's performance, tolerance of frustration, capacity to wait, the influence of third parties (teammates, coach, public), as well as a certain persistence in the attainment of one's goals.

It can be said that when players go out on the pitch they are often loaded, not only with their own expectations and ambitions but also with those of their family, which can burden economic and sport achievements. Moreover this can include the expectations of a whole town or nation, who appoint their athletes as representatives of their land, customs, and way of life—a diplomatic role that players often willingly accept. For all these reasons, strong ambivalent feelings often arise that can "betray" the player in the attainment of his conscious goal (winning). Some players may confront these moments with more harmony, a result of their experience, capacity, strength, and group support. But many others will require psychological training and elaboration that will allow them to get through demands and conflicts without injuring themselves.

We know for a fact that what is not processed at the psychological level will derive from the player's body or conduct as the voice of protest or alarm before demands that prove excessive. As highlighted previously, repeated injuries are the perfect means of expressing conflicts that otherwise wouldn't find a way of channelling themselves. It's the forced way of stopping, of saying "that's enough". It's more socially acceptable than showing "psychological weakness", which is understood as the need for help and collaboration to solve anguish or pressures that are overwhelming and definitely suffered by athletes but generally not admitted.

All that has been previously mentioned applies not only to proven anatomical injuries but also to (very frequent) functional disorders like spasms, cramps, painful contractions, and even the tearing of muscles. In these cases, it is customary to say, in non-academic terms, that the athlete doesn't want to play, that he or she is afraid, that there's nothing wrong with him or her. But in fact something *is* wrong; we're dealing with an emotional issue that impacts on the body. It's the athlete's way of showing he or she is affected, regardless of what is consciously declared. It's very important that those close to the athlete understand this aspect in order to point him or her in the direction of appropriate (psychological) attention, instead of making unnecessary value judgements; these are usually strong personal attacks, which only manage to favour dissociative mechanisms, generating further isolation, overload, and suffering.

I have observed players of different sports who injured themselves while being overseas, generally alone, as a way of channelling feelings like homesickness, or missing loved ones (partner, family members).

The injury allowed them to return home to their dear ones. Of course it would have been much more beneficial, not only financially but at the psychological, bodily and sport levels, to express what was happening at the affective level and thus try to prevent a more harmful outcome. The possibility of working psychologically can prevent, guide and clarify problems in athletes as well as relieve the burden that falls on the family, the technical staff and healthcare team, who rely on their human capacity but cannot provide the appropriate professional help required to deal with these issues.

It often happens that athletes demonstrate an over-adaptation to the reality of their surroundings, which implies a high level of subjugation to the demands and requirements of their environment. This is further enhanced by the important rewards they obtain. Little space can be spared for aesthetic or playful enjoyment, the pleasure of movement, and there is even less space for emotions like sadness, loneliness, or anguish. The emphasis on results, which we observe so much nowadays, measures everything in terms of efficiency, almost as if athletes were machines meant to produce successful results, with those proving the most suitable the ones who manage to dissociate themselves the most, without feeling or thinking too much. The price of these mechanisms is a greater degree of somatic vulnerability, manifesting itself many times in the form of injuries. For others, drugs are the escape from that psychic suffering, allowing them to withstand and endure the demands placed on them, but at a much higher cost.

FURTHER READING

Cohen, M. N., & Rubinstein, R. (1993). Lo inconciente en el deporte. Presented at Symposium, APA.

Freud, S. (1911b). Formulations on the two principles of mental functioning. S. E. *12*: 218–238.

Freud, S. (1913i). The disposition to obsessional neurosis. S. E. 12.

Freud, S. (1920g). *Beyond the Pleasure Principle*. S. E. 18.

Freud, S. (1926d). *Inhibitions, Symptoms and Anxiety*. S. E. 20.

Guiter, M. (1991). Sublimación. *Revista de Psicoanálisis*, APA, *17*: 4.

Jones, E. (1953–1957). *The Life and Work of Sigmund Freud*. New York: Basic Books.

Rubinstein, R. (2003). Placer del movimiento, competencia y deporte. *Revista de Psiconanálisis*, APA, *11*: 2.

Santoro, R. (2007). *Literatura de la pelota*. Buenos Aires: Lea Editorial.

REFERENCES

Abadi, M. (1963). Psicoanálisis del jugar. *Revista de Psicoanálisis*, APA, *20*.

Alizade, M. (1966). Desamparo y dominio, senderos pulsionales e inferencias clínicas. *Revista de Psicoanálisis*, APA, Número especial Internacional, *5*.

Archetti, E. (2003). *Masculinidades, fútbol, tango y polo en la Argentina*. Buenos Aires: Antropofagia.

Avenburg, R. (1999). La acción desde la perspectiva psicoanalítica. *Teoría de la acción*, Buenos Aires, Asociación Argentina de Epistemología del Psicoanálisis.

Baranger, M. & Baranger, W. (1993). El enfoque económico en psicoanálisis. In: *Problemas del campo psicoanalítico*. Buenos Aires: Kargieman.

Baranger, M., Baranger, W., & Mom, J. M. (1988). The infantile psychic trauma from us to Freud: Pure trauma, retroactivity and reconstruction. *International Journal of Psycho-Analysis, 69*: 113–128.

Bleger, J., Churcher J., & Bleger L. (Eds.) (1978). *Symbiosis and Ambiguity: A Psychoanalytic Study*. Buenos Aires: Paidos [reprinted London: Routledge, 2013].

Bleichmar, H. (1981). *El narcisismo, estudio sobre la enunciación y la gramática inconsciente*. Buenos Aires: Nueva Visión.

Boecker, H. (2008). The runner's high, opioidergic mechanisms in the human brain. *Cerebral Cortex, 18*(11): 2523–2531.

Browning, J. (2012). Sydney stops to honour Olympians. *ABC Grandstand Sport*, 20 August. Available at: www.abc.net.au/news/2012-08-20/sydney-stops-to-give-olympians-a-warm-welcome/4210184 [last accessed 25 April 2016].

Bull, A. (2008). Olympics: Isinbayeva raises the bar and the Bird's Nest roof. *Guardian*, 19 August. Available at: www.theguardian.com/sport/2008/aug/19/olympics2008.olympicsathletics3 [last accessed 25 April 2016].

Caillois, R. (1958). *Man, Play and Games*. Paris: Librairie Gallimard [reprinted University of Illinois Press, 1961].

Daily Mail. (2011). Hero's welcome! Djokovic greeted by 100,000 fans as Serbia salutes the Wimbledon champion. 5 July. Available at: www.dailymail.co.uk/sport/tennis/article-2011350/Novak-Djokovic-returns-Belgrade-greeted-100-000-fans.html#ixzz3YvrHqpPK [last accessed 22 April 2016].

D'Alvia, R. (1995). El cuerpo en psicoanálisis. *Revista de Psicoanálisis*, APA, Número especial Internacional, 4.

Davies, C. (2012). London 2012 medallists welcomed by the Queen to Buckingham Palace. *Guardian*, 23 October. Available at: www.theguardian.com/sport/2012/oct/23/london-2012-medallists-buckingham-palace [last accessed 22 April 2016].

De Castro, A. L. (1998). Culto al cuerpo, modernidad y medios de comunicación. *Efdeportes*. Available at: www.efdeportes.com/efd9/anae.htm [last accessed 25 April 2016].

Del Valle Echegaray, E., & Moise de Borgnia, C. (1996). Psicoanálisis y poder. *Revista de Psicoanálisis*, APA, Número especial Internacional, 5.

Deutsch, H. (1926). A contribution to the psychology of sport. *International Journal of Psychoanalysis, 7*: 223–227.

Devries, O. (2004). La ola que salvó a Gaudio. *La Nación*, 22 June. Available at: www.lanacion.com.ar/612101-la-ola-que-salvo-a-gaudio [last accessed 25 April 2016].

Dishman, R., Berthoud, H. R., & Booth, F. W. et al. (2006). Neurobiology of exercise. *Obesity, 14*(3): 345–356.

Fenichel, O. (1945). *The Psychoanalytic Theory of Neurosis*. New York: W. W. Norton & Company [reprinted London: Routledge and Kegan, 1946].

Freud, S. (1888–1889). Preface to the translation of Bernheim's Suggestion. S. E. *1*: 73.

Freud, S. (1895d). *Studies on Hysteria*. S. E. 2.

Freud, S. (1905d). *Three Essays on the Theory of Sexuality*. S. E. *7*: 125.

Freud, S. (1912b). The dynamics of transference. S. E. *12*: 97–107.

Freud, S. (1912–1913). *Totem and Taboo*. S. E. *13*: 1–161.

Freud, S. (1913c). On beginning the treatment. S. E. *12*: 121–144.

Freud, S. (1915c). Instincts and their vicissitudes. S. E. 14.

Freud, S. (1923b). *The Ego and the Id*. S. E. 19.

Freud, S. (1927c). *The Future of an Illusion*. S. E. 21: 3.

Freud, S. (1930a). *Civilization and its Discontents*. S. E. 21: 59.

Galeano, E. (2000). *El fútbol a sol y a sombra*. España: Siglo XXI.

Green, A. (2001). *Life Narcissism, Death Narcissism*. London: Free Association Books.

Groisman, R. (2007). Maratón, cerebro y psicoanálisis. Presented at Expo Maraton, Buenos Aires, 2007.

Halfon, M. (2007). El malestar nuestro de cada día, la violencia en el fútbol. Presented at APA, 2007.

Hughes, G. (2015). Feel-good warriors now under enormous pressure to win NBA title. *Bleacher Report*, April 2015. Available at: bleacherreport.com/articles/2424386-feel-good-warriors-now-under-enormous-pressure-to-win-nba-title [last accessed 22 April 2016].

Huizinga, J. (1949). *Homo Ludens: A Study of the Play Element in Culture* [reprinted London: Routledge and Kegan, 2002].

Issaharoff, E. (1999). Psicoanálisis, mente y acción. *Teoría de la acción*, Buenos Aires, ADEP.

Johnson, S. (2013). Petr Cech feeling pressure to end on high. *London Evening Standard*, 22 April. Available at: www.standard.co.uk/sport/football/petr-cech-feeling-pressure-to-end-on-high-8582880.html [last accessed 22 April 2016].

Journal of the American Medical Association (JAMA). (2008). Sedentary lifestyles associated with accelerated aging process. *ScienceDaily*, 29 January. Available at: www.sciencedaily.com/releases/2008/01/080128165734.htm [last accessed 25 April 2016].

Kancyper, L. (1998). *El complejo fraterno* [reprinted Buenos Aires: Lumen, 2004].

Kessel, A. (2012). London 2012: Meeting Steve Ovett has inspired me, says Andrew Osagie. *Guardian*, 20 June. Available at: www.theguardian.com/sport/2012/jun/20/london-2012-steve-ovett-andrew-osagie [last accessed 25 April 2016].

Klein, M. (1929). Personification in the play of children. In: *Love, Guilt and Reparation and Other Works (1921–1945): The Writings of Melanie Klein. Vol 1*: 199–209. London: Hogarth Press [reprinted London: Karnac, 1992].

Kohut, H. (1977). *The Restoration of the Self*. University of Chicago Press.

La Nación. (2008a). Espero que la derrota no nos pegue fuerte, 11 August. Available at: www.lanacion.com.ar/1038486-espero-que-la-derrota-no-nos-pegue-fuerte [last accessed 25 May 2016].

La Nación. (2008b). A very demanding mom, 18 August 2008.

Landolfi, P. (1998). La culpa fraterna, una nueva estructuración del superyó. *Revista de Psicoanálisis*, APA, 1.

Marty, P., & de M'Uzan, M. (1963). Operational thinking. In: D. Birksted-Braen, S. Flanders, & A. Gibeault (Eds). *Reading French Psychoanalysis*. Hove: Routledge, 2010.

Menayo, D. (2007). Hingis: No pienso en la retirada, sigo entrenando duro. *Marca*, 26 September. Available at: archivo.marca.com/edicion/marca/tenis/es/desarrollo/1039962.html [last accessed 25 May 2016].

Pagani, H. (2006). *El fútbol que le gusta a la gente*. Buenos Aires: Al Arco.

Pichon Riviere, E. (2007). *Literatura de la pelota*. Buenos Aires: Lea Editorial.

Rodríguez, F. F. (n.d). Estadoy Deporte. www.portalfitness.com/articulos/educación_fisica/estadoydeporte.htm [webpage now defunct].

Ronaldo7.net. (2011). 3 September. Available at: www.ronaldo7.net/news/archive/269-cristiano-ronaldo-i-answer-fans-booing-in-the-pitch.html [last accessed 25 May 2016].

Rubinstein, R. (1998). Ataque de pánico, visión psicoanalítica. Presented at FEPAL Congress, Cartagena de Indias, Colombia, 1998.

Torres, D. (2008). La vanguardia del Caribe. *El País*, 8 September. Available at: elpais.com/diario/2008/09/08/deportes/1220824812_850215.html [last accessed 25 May 2016].

Trenado, J. M. (2008). Ahora a reinventarse. *La Nación*, 18 August. Available at: www.lanacion.com.ar/1040763-ahora-a-reinventarse [last accessed 30 May 2016].

Vázquez Montalbán, M. (1972). *Cien años de deporte*. Barcelona: Difusora Internacional.

Winnicott, D. W. (1969). Positive and negative aspects of psychosomatic disease. *Rev Med Psychosom Psychol Med*, 11(2): 205–216.

Winnicott, D. W. (1972). *Playing and Reality*. London: Tavistock.

INDEX

For Product Safety Concerns and Information please contact our EU
representative GPSR@taylorandfrancis.com Taylor & Francis Verlag GmbH,
Kaufingerstraße 24, 80331 München, Germany

Batch number: 08153785

Printed by Printforce, the Netherlands